A Daily Gift of Peace

A COLLECTION OF STORIES FROM
HEARTS UNITED IN PEACE
FROM AROUND THE GLOBE

Teresa Velardi

Daily Gift Books
Authentic Endeavors Publishing Scranton, PA
dailygiftbookseries@gmail.com

Interior Design by Amit Dey

A Daily Gift of Peace
ISBN: 978-1-967041-38-1 (Paperback)
        978-1-967041-39-8 (eBook)

St. Francis of Assisi: Make Me an Instrument of Your Peace

Lord, make me an instrument of your peace.
Where there is hatred, let me sow love;
where there is injury, pardon;
where there is doubt, faith;
where there is despair, hope;
where there is darkness, light;
and where there is sadness, joy.

O Divine Master, grant that I may not so much seek
to be consoled as to console;
to be understood as to understand;
to be loved as to love.
For it is in giving that we receive;
it is in pardoning that we are pardoned;
and it is in dying that we are born to eternal life.
Amen.

Peace is its own reward.

Mahatma Gandhi

Let There Be Peace on Earth

by Jill Jackson and Sy Miller

Let there be peace on earth And let it begin with me; Let there be peace on earth, The peace that was meant to be.

With God as our Father

Brothers all are we,

Let me walk with my brother In perfect harmony.

Let peace begin with me,

Let this be the moment now; With every step I take, Let this be my solemn vow:

To take each moment and live each moment In peace eternally. Let there be peace on earth And let it begin with me.

Dedication

To all who seek the comfort of peace. Whether you have found it, shared it, or are still looking for it, may the stories that follow open your heart to enrich or help to fill your desire for peace.

To Karen Mayfield, who celebrates her birthday on September 21, World Peace Day. We shared my first radio show experience on your Blogtalk Radio show on World Peace Day about 15 years ago. That was the beginning of an adventure filled with unknowns, lots of laughs, great friendships, and hope for peace, particularly, Peace of Mind. You have enriched my life experience in so many ways. I'm grateful to be able to call you "friend."

Happy World Peace Day Birthday!

Peace is in Our Hands

Table of Contents

Acknowledgments

I'm grateful for each of the authors whose stories are part of this compilation. Your voices speak clearly and profoundly.

Peggy Willms, you are a steadfast, loyal friend and helper on this Daily Gift journey. Thank you for all you do.

Aljon Inertia, you have been and continue to be an immense blessing. Your talent is unsurpassed!

Mary Vovers Brown, your support through this project has been a true gift. Thank you for all you do for and with this series. You are a blessing.

GOOD

Things

ARE GOING

To

HAPPEN

Foreword

Peace

by Andi Buerger JD

If ever there was a time when weary hearts, burdened souls, and humanity in general needed to regain a state of wholeness and restoration, it is at this moment. Freedom from oppressive circumstances, troublesome thoughts, encumbered emotions, and societal trepidations keep individuals and communities from being able to thrive without constraints.

A Daily Gift of Peace brings an exceptional collection of real stories from authors all around the world who share their personal truths and insights. Each narrative on the pages of this book helps readers to discover precious life nuggets such as harmony in personal relationships, rest for anxious souls, faith to press on in desperate circumstances, and inspiration to become peacemakers in their own circles of influence.

Genuine peace requires more than just removing conflict. It requires getting to the root of conflict - personal, relational, cultural, societal - and learning to live in harmony with ourselves and with others. As that happens, our inner spirits can purposely focus on the present and experience unpretentious joy in everyday life. Sometimes, it really is the simple things in life that bring rest for the soul and peace to our hearts and minds.

Some claim that peace is an elusive fantasy, not unlike a precious jewel that millions want to own because its value is priceless. Some will claim that peace can even be bought (or sold). For me, it has been an ongoing pursuit since conception. Seriously. Yet that early desperation and pursuit is what ultimately drove me to achieve a quiet stillness in my heart, the release of control to my Heavenly Father, and the ability to create better boundaries and healthier responses to anything that sought to disturb my overall peace. One could say I have "earned my stripes" in the battle for personal, spiritual, and relational peace.

By the time I was 18 months old, I had already been routinely violated by immediate and extended family members. It was a time when people did not speak about unseemly activities. Children were regarded more as chattel than as viable, beautiful beings delivered as human angels from God above to those who would be responsible for molding their young hearts and lives.

At age 5, this 'human angel' sat on the curb of her house waiting for a car to come by. I wanted to jump in front of it so I could no longer be tortured, violated, humiliated, and passed around to others who did the same thing. If I were dead, no one could touch me, and at least I would be at peace. As I waited to end my life at five, God met me on that curb. The voice I heard in my heart said, "This is not the plan I have for you. Suicide is not the answer." I was stunned that anyone knew what I was trying to do! Yet, the gentle, peace-filled resonance of His voice made this terrified tiny child take a leap of faith and trust it. "If you keep me alive, I'll do whatever you *call* me to do." Big statement for a little girl. Four decades later, that calling would manifest itself into a voice that now speaks to nations on behalf of God's children.

From that point, my life was still threatened, still broken, and absolutely without peace. I chose to believe God's voice was bigger than the people who hurt me. The brother who tried to smother me to death had left home when I was 17, which was also the last time my birth mother tried to kill me. As I started college, I finally began to see how other people lived. My world was opening up, but I felt terrified every single day. I woke up wondering if someone would "find out" the truth of my life, if someone else would hurt me, or try to get too close to me emotionally. I was a shattered life and a ticking time bomb to some extent. There were no agencies or safehouses for such situations during my early and young adult years. It was one of the reasons I put myself through law school. I wanted a way to help kids who had been hurt like I had, though I later realized how prejudicial the judicial system was when it came to advocating and protecting children of all ages. Business became my focus, and if I was successful, I could help any child I chose.

Fast forward to a dark and abusive marriage, which ended in divorce and a move to Oregon from California. At 35, it was a huge transition, and I had no idea how I would start over - again. I had made a promise to God when I married, and now it was shattered. God answered my unspoken plea for peace and calm as I rebuilt my life. He sent me *Streams In The Desert* through a friend. I didn't know it at the time, but those traditional daily devotions were the *first steps to my peace journey*. Every page gave me food for thought and something for my trampled soul to ponder, just in bite-sized pieces.

As a classic overachiever and growing child of God, I accomplished amazing things. Despite the accolades and success, there was something I still lacked - inner peace. As I pursued God and experienced His love tangibly, not just intellectually, "the" moment soon arrived. God nudged me at first, but then it became a little more direct: *Forgive them.* In my head, I heard myself say, "What? I can't do that! After all they did to me, why?" In my heart, I already knew the answer: *Because it's for my good, not theirs.* Our Heavenly Father is a good dad. He is patient with His creation, especially *me*. I resisted, and finally my heart gave in. "I can't do it. You will have to do it through me." God did.

Eventually, I released and forgave every single predator in my life. By forgiving them, I was now free. Free to receive God's blessings, free to live my life the way I wanted to, and free to experience peace. It resulted in more peaceful thoughts and more peace-filled nights.

Not everything was perfect, but at least I knew what genuine peace could feel like. *God was right.* Imagine that.

Moving forward, I looked for ways to find peace on a regular basis. When I married my husband of twenty-five plus years now, I had perfect peace that God had provided this amazing human who took me lock, stock, and barrel because it was His gift to me. Life has had tremendous trials and adversities and joys and wonders ever since. What I know from six plus decades of life is that we may always have to readjust or reposition our 'peace meter' as circumstances arise. The important thing is that we never give up the pursuit. I can honestly say that there *is* joy in the journey. Then again, I am a tenacious redhead who never understood the word 'quit' in her life.

Teresa Velardi is an extraordinary publisher, successful author, entrepreneur, and friend. To me, she is 100% hero! Someone right now is struggling with whether they can ever have peace in their life. They can. One of these personal narratives could be the key or at least a beginning to the necessary pursuit. *The Daily Gift* series provides readers with content that will enlighten, engage, and encourage positivity and rising hope as each page is turned.

If a book like *A Daily Gift of Peace* had been available in my early years, maybe I would not have felt so alone in the fight for intentional rest in my soul, body, and mind. At least I would have known that I wasn't the only one desperate for the promise and presence of inner peace.

Introduction

In a world that often feels hurried and divided, the simple yet profound gift of peace can sometimes seem just out of reach. Yet, peace is not a distant ideal reserved for a select few—it is a daily offering, quietly waiting to be embraced in the moments of our lives.

A Daily Gift of Peace brings together voices from every corner of the globe, a tapestry of stories woven from hearts united in their yearning for peace. This collection is a celebration of humanity's shared desire to find calm in chaos, hope in hardship, and connection beyond boundaries.

Each contributor offers a unique glimpse into their personal journey—stories of healing, courage, kindness, and transformation. Through their words, you will encounter the gentle power of peace manifesting in everyday acts, in struggles overcome, and in the deep well of compassion that binds us all.

As you turn these pages, may you find inspiration and comfort. May these stories remind you that peace is not just a destination but a living presence within each of us—waiting to be discovered anew every day.

Together, let us open our hearts and receive this daily gift of peace

You'll never find peace of mind until you listen to your heart.

George Michael

Wake Up Women!
It's Karen Mayfield...
by Kathleen O'Keefe-Kanavos
Kat-The Queen of Dreams

When Teresa Velardi, Wake Up Women author and publisher, said she was dedicating this book to Karen Mayfield for Karen's birthday and World Peace Day, and invited me to write a bit about Karen, I was honored. So, here goes... Karen Mayfield! To know her is to love her. The End!

Yup, just the name Karen Mayfield is a whole story. But here's a bit more, so if you don't already know and love her, you can, too.

Fifteen years ago, on World Peace Day 2010, I joined a Zoom call led by Karen Mayfield, owner of **Wake Up Women**. Although I had no knowledge of this group, Karen, or what **WUW** stood for, I intuitively joined the call that changed my life. Karen was energy incarnate. Her contagious laughter greeted each new person like an old friend. Everyone belonged.

Minutes into the call she said in her southern drawl, "I just read the most amazin' book, Pope Annalisa by Peter Canova, 'bout a nun who becomes pope. Anyone know the book or him?"
Silence. "Anyone?" Crickets....
"Ummm, yeah. I do." I finally answered.
"Really?" Karen exclaimed. "You read it?"
"Many times, while being written. Peter Canova's my husband."
"No way!"

'Yeah! Wanna talk to him? He's right here listening."
And that is how WUW met Peter, and I joined a group of forever-friends.

Later that year WUW met at Karen's sprawling horse ranch in Arkansas. Many of us were strangers who quickly discovered a reconnected sisterhood. While Karen's pet goat tried to poke us in the butt or chase us up a fence, Teresa Velardi, Suzanne Strisower, Karen Mayfield, and I, part of the core group, spent HOURS planning, sharing, and laughing while we grew closer and planned Wake Up Women's future. Our personal stories bonded us. The words, "Like a broom!" still send us into fits of laughter from when Karen recounted leaving the top down through a self-serve carwash while yelling at "those darn kids!" Her soap-soaked hair, blowing in the wind, stood straight out like stiff broom bristles from the side of her head as she drove home. "Like a Broom!" became our war cry for laughter whenever "S*#T Happened."

WUW held events and published books that brought empowerment to women worldwide. Goal accomplished! Thank you, Karen Mayfield, for being our fearless leader.

Karen Mayfield! To know her is to love her. The End.

A Peaceful Glimpse of Heaven

by Teresa Velardi

After years of lung cancer treatments, a brief remission, and more procedures than anyone should endure—chemotherapy, hospitalizations, even brain surgery—Mom was tired. She met every challenge with grace; the rest of us, not so much. There was always talk of the "next option," the newest trial, another surgery. My fearful siblings wanted to keep trying.

At one last consultation, the doctor described another procedure to delay the inevitable. I saw it in Mom's eyes: "I'm done." I thanked the doctor, wheeled her to the elevator, and took her home. No more treatment. Mom was at peace. I was, too. My siblings came around as she stood her ground.

Even as her body failed, Mom's spirit sparkled. Hospice settled in. Much of the time, it was just the two of us. She rested in her recliner, eyes closed as the TV murmured, or drifting through memories. Dad had died a decade earlier, and she spoke of him more than usual. I felt sure he was near.

"How are you doing, Mom? Do you need anything?" I asked.

"I'm tired, Teresa," she said. "It's almost time. I know where I'm going, and I'm ready. I'm going to miss you."

I told her she would always live in my heart, and that I'd see her again. My faith lets me say that with confidence. She had an undeniable sense of peace about her.

Family members arrived to say their goodbyes. Mom drifted in and out, naming people she still wanted to see, and most came that day.

That night, as I tucked her in, she was distracted, fixing her gaze on the corner where the ceiling met the wall. I tried to draw her back, but she was watching something, then began to giggle.

"Okay, Mom," I said, "who's here?"

One by one, she named our deceased relatives. Her face glowed. "They're cooking the pasta for the party," she said. "I'm going home." Joy radiated from her. I'd heard stories like this, but now I saw it in her eyes—a miracle.

She slept peacefully. The next morning, we learned my brother's family was on the way. All day, Mom drifted as nurses came and went. Then my brother arrived. When I told her, her eyes flew open. "Get me up! I want to get up!"

We dressed her, then wheeled her to the kitchen. She came alive—eating, laughing, and playing with the great-grandkids, taking in every moment. She even played cards. If you'd told me that morning this would happen, I would've said you were out of your mind. But there she was, awake, aware, alive—another miracle.

That night, I prayed she could see the last few people she'd named, especially her beloved doctor. Again, she slept peacefully.

The next day, Mom was mostly unresponsive. When Doctor B. arrived, my sister and nieces tried to wake her. When they couldn't, I took Mom's hands and called, "MA!" She turned, looked me in the eyes, and said, "What?"

"Doctor B. is here," I said. Mom's face lit up. I propped her up and listened as she thanked the doctor for years of attentive care. Even at the edge of her final breath, Mom spoke with gratitude. She was and will always be the most courageous woman I know.

Her breathing grew labored as Doctor B. comforted her, told her it was okay to go. We kept her comfortable, wrapped in family love, until later that day she slipped peacefully from this world into the loving arms of Jesus.

A few days later, we gathered for her celebration of life. A friend with the gift of "seeing" pulled me aside. "Your mom and dad are standing at the head of the casket," she said. "They want to thank you for the sendoff. They look so happy together." Another blessing.

I was given one more gift: the strength to deliver the eulogy. I said simply that we loved her, that Mom taught us family is larger than blood, that friendships can last a lifetime, that faith in God and one another carries us through, and that courage looks like living fully in the face of loss. The church was packed, evidence of how many lives she'd touched.

I heard my great-nephew's words from the front row: "Grandma is with Poppie now, telling him about me, my sister, and my baby brother." I faltered there, then found my voice. "Mom may not be here in body, but she lives in our hearts. This isn't goodbye; it's 'til we meet again.' Aunt Rose never said goodbye; she'd say, 'I love you, and God bless you.' So that's what I'll say now: I love you, Mom. God bless you." So many years later, I find peace in remembering the moment when, through my mother's eyes, I received a little glimpse of heaven.

May the God of hope fill you with
all joy and peace.

Romans 15:13

Peace is a Gift-Not a Goal

by Alysia Lyons

As a mom and a healer, I've learned that peace isn't something we find—it's something we *create*. It's not a reward for having it all together, but a practice we return to, especially when things feel undone.

Peace lives in the exhale after the tantrum, in the silence between appointments, in the sacred seconds where I remember I don't have to carry it all. It shows up in the soft moments when I choose presence over pressure, and grace over guilt.

It's easy to believe that peace will come when the house is clean, the to-do list is done, or everyone else is happy. But peace doesn't wait for perfection. It waits for permission. And we are the ones who get to give it.

We cultivate peace when we speak gently to ourselves, even when we don't get it right. When we honor our energy, set loving boundaries, and hold space for both tears and laughter. As people, we pour out so much—but peace reminds us to pour back in.

Let today be the day you choose peace, not because everything is calm, but because *you* are worthy of calm. You don't need to earn it. You simply need to receive it—like a soft hand on your heart, a warm breath in your belly, a quiet whisper that says: "You're doing enough. You *are* enough."

That is the daily gift of peace.

The Peace Plant

by Mary Vovers Brown

In a city of glass towers and concrete sidewalks, where steel met sky and sirens were more common than silence, a single green sprout pushed up through a crack by the subway entrance. Most people rushed past. Eyes on screens. Ears plugged in. Lives too loud. No one noticed it, except Isabella. She was eight, with curious eyes, a head full of stars, and a heart full of questions. Every morning, she paused to water the tiny plant with drops from her lunch bottle. She named it Hope.

Soon, other kids joined in. A soda can became a planter. Seeds were tucked into the soil and gently tended. A teenager painted flowers on the grey wall. Passersby began to smile. They slowed down. A businessman offered old pots. A woman brought herbs from home. Strangers, once silent, began to talk. Someone added handwritten words to the wall: "Peace Grows Here." And it did. Sometimes, all it takes to soften a city is one stubborn seed - and a child who believes in magic.

Peace I leave with you; my peace I give you.

John 14:27

His Peace is My Peace

by Dr. Anne Worth

I had no peace, but I wanted it desperately. I searched for it, meditated on it, and read about it, but never found it for more than a few minutes.

Pull yourself up by your bootstraps, Anne. You are responsible for attaining what you want. If you don't have what you want, it's your fault. What was wrong with me? Regardless of what I did, I remained in a state of stress and worry.

I had never liked God. I blamed Him for all the bad in the world, but I heard other people talk about His peace.

I wondered, *What dramatic thing does one have to do to get in God's good graces?* Surely, I would have to fall on my knees and beg for forgiveness.

Just out of earshot, I heard the words: "Decide He is real and ask for help." Decide? That seemed way too simple to be true!Expecting nothing, I told this imaginary God that I was defeated and needed help. As soon as the words were out of my mouth, it felt like someone wrapped a soft, warm blanket around me. Something happened! Was it God?

The answer is yes!

In one miraculous, unbelievable moment, I experienced the comfort of a loving God. Nothing in my mind or heart has ever been the same since that electric moment. When I gave up, He lifted me up.

May the God of peace be with you all.

Romans 15:33

My Greatest Speech

by Kevin Stark

It was finally time. Twelve men gathered for a Rites of Passage event in the mountains. Upon arrival, they were given instructions to hike to the meeting point: a rocky cliff overlooking the valley below. I waited there for them. Rehearsing and practicing words that would move men's souls. Visions of Viking eloquence fused with Sitting Bull's wisdom danced in my mind. I wrote and rewrote words in my notebook as birds trumpeted my triumphant presence to the trees.

Swelling with confidence, I reverently closed my notebook so as not to disturb the aura of my mountain-top address.

Feeling ready, I took a moment to be still.

In my stillness, I heard the wisdom of the wind make its way up the cliffs.

In my stillness, I saw the patience of the sun on its track to the horizon.

In my stillness, I felt the power of the mountain under my feet.

In my stillness, I was aware.

In my awareness, I understood.

I understood that my words would only dull the sublime perfection of the present moment.

The first lesson of the retreat was for me.

My words, my speech, my ego had no place on the mountain.

I smiled, put my notebook in my backpack, and sat peacefully.

The guys arrived a few minutes later. I could hear them before I could see them. They approached each other, talking excitedly and energized to be on an adventure.

I greeted them with a handshake and the greatest speech I have ever given: "Let's sit here for a minute and watch the sunset."

Each man found a spot and together, in silence, we watched the sun do what it does best: be.

For God is not a God of disorder but of peace.

1 Corinthians 14:33

Becoming A Vessel Of Peace
by Amanda Beth Johnson

The world is swirling with urgency, unrest, and headlines that can overwhelm the heart. In times like these, it's easy to absorb the collective storm and forget your quiet power. Yet, it's precisely in this noise that your inner peace becomes a sacred act of courage.

Peace is not passive—it's a conscious choice, an energetic reclamation. Amid outside chaos, you have the strength to return again and again to your center, your sacred sovereignty. Every time you pause, breathe, and soften, you choose a different rhythm than the world's hurried drum.

When the weight of the collective presses heavy, it becomes the calm within the storm:

- Let your breath anchor you.
- Place a gentle hand on your heart and feel its steady beat.
- In the presence of pain or fear, allow yourself to soften rather than harden.

As an intuitive healer, I see how inner steadiness radiates outward. One person's calm energy becomes an invisible haven for others—a silent offering, a lighthouse guiding weary souls home. Remember, you are not here to shoulder the world's pain—you are here to transform it, moment by moment, with intention and compassion.

Ask yourself:

- What would it mean to incorporate peace today, even for just one moment?

- Where can I invite softness into the discomfort that rises?

Let your nervous system be a sanctuary. Allow your presence to become an invitation to peace. Perfection is not the goal; wholeheartedness is.

When more individuals choose peace—imperfectly, authentically— the energy of the world begins to shift—your energy matters. Your presence of peace is a gift.

Today, may you stand as a vessel of calming peace amid the world's waves, trusting that your gentle light is needed now more than ever.

A Prayer for Peace in the World

Author Unknown

God, it seems that every time I turn on the news,
the world gets a little worse each day.
I know sin has ravaged this planet and that the world
will lack complete peace until you return.
Nevertheless, I ask that you intervene in the
world and grant us peace.
Help us find more ways to love our neighbors
and show the world
your goodness.
Amen.

September 21 is World Peace Day

Please share this prayer with those you love
and pray for all those who need love.

Do not be anxious about anything,
but in every situation,
by prayer and petition, with thanksgiving,
make your needs known to God.
And the peace of God, which transcends
all understanding,
will guard your hearts and minds through
Christ Jesus.

Philippians 4:6-7 (NIV)

Peace

by Sherry Martin Peters

*Peace. It does not mean to be in a place where there is no noise,
trouble, or hard work. It means to be in the midst of all those
things and still be calm in your heart.*
Unknown

In a chaotic world, so many are searching for peace, but what is the key to achieving deep-rooted peace?

True peace comes from completely surrendering control to and trusting in God to settle our inner turmoil. When we give our worries, struggles, and anxieties to God, His presence remains our constant anchor. Peace is His promise that you will never have to face life's challenges alone. It calls you to let go of your burdens and replace them with the assurance of God's love and guidance. The moment you truly give it all to Him, you start to realize a unique inner calm, a peace that defies explanation until you have experienced it for yourself.

Finding peace through God is a journey of opening your heart, surrendering your worries, and nurturing a personal relationship with Him. How do you do that?

1. Cultivate a Prayerful Life. Don't only ask for solutions but also listen and share your heart with God.

2. Immerse Yourself in the Bible: It offers wisdom by reminding you of God's promises and unfailing presence.

3. Practice Surrender: Trust that God's plan is greater than your current circumstances.

be
happy

Gratitude vs. Sorrow

by Angela Bertone

For most of my life, I have lived a life of gratitude and felt grateful nearly every day. Don't misunderstand; of course, I was sad at times, like we all are, but I would have described myself as a happy person with a lot to be grateful for.

Being thought of as a happy person was my norm until it was my turn to see myself in a different light. The kind of light that is only found in our darkest moments. I had no idea that everyone suffers greatly sometimes. Sadness, anger, betrayal, rejection, and such are common to us, and that is not the kind of sorrow I am speaking of. I am talking about the kind of sorrow that I thought would never happen to me; you know, the kind of sorrow that you think only happens to other people.

I had no idea there was a place inside of me that could suffer so much that at times I found myself unable to function. In time, however, I learned to endure and spent what seemed like an eternity just surviving, but that was about it, just surviving. In fact, I felt paralyzed and wanted out. I did not want to take my life, but I did want God to come and get me and take me home. I could not imagine living a long life of endurance.

Day by day, I learned to live through my sorrow, and I also learned how to grow from my painful experiences. One morning, my husband brought me coffee in bed. He propped up my pillow, snuggled in next to me, and then reached over to the nightstand and gingerly passed my coffee cup and took up his, pretending to sip it while it was still too hot, bragging on how good his coffee was. It was being present in moments like this that allowed me to temporarily forget my sorrows. We were really good at stretching out the time we spent in bed sipping our coffee. Waking up together, laughing, picking, and flirting with each other was our favorite excuse to take our coffee time beyond slow.

After I finished my cup, I crawled over him and reached to set my cup back on the nightstand, grinning and knowing he would find another chance to flirt and play when my eyes caught a glimpse of it. It was my son's picture. He was smiling and playing intimately with his dad. He was about 14 in that picture, full of life and promise. My heart sank with a loud thud deep in my soul as I was reminded of all that addiction had taken from him and us.

In that instant, my tears began to flow as I found my way back to my spot on the bed and buried my face in my husband's shoulder. I was no longer in the present joy. I was remembering the past and fearing the future. My husband saw what happened and understood as together we had already been suffering for nearly 10 years. As I lay weeping, I heard God say, "Does your sorrow rob you of the joy you shared this morning?" I replied, "No, Father, I love our mornings together." Does the joy you shared this morning deliver you from your sorrow?" Again, I replied, "No, Father, it does not." He said, "Not many are able to learn how to live and have both exist. My children often think only one or the other is possible. You have learned how to live and experience both without losing your joy." I replied, "Thank You, Father, Thank You!"

Being grateful is the bridge to peace in the moments of sorrow and or fear come knocking. May our story remind you in the darkest of moments that joy still exists, and gratitude for what is, is the pathway through because escape is only an illusion.

Finding Peace Through the Unknown
Aljon Comahig

Just before my 18th birthday, I was diagnosed with heart enlargement, inherited from my father. It was the worst and darkest time of my life. I could barely walk, breathed heavily, and couldn't sleep without pillows piled behind my back to elevate my chest.

With no plan, dream, or intention to fight, I wondered, "Will I die?" How could I find peace with not knowing, especially when my parents couldn't answer that question? My days were routine: sleep, rest, watch the sunset, and wait for the moon to rise.

One day, while searching for entertainment on my computer. I stumbled upon a Japanese anime artist. Drawn to his art, I enjoyed reading the stories one episode each day!

Though I didn't have experience with drawing or art of any kind, I decided to learn from online videos. Though frustrated, I felt challenged to draw. I decided I wanted to be an artist, but I had to live longer to do that.

I prayed every day. "Lord God, if you have no intention of taking my life, please help me become an artist. I want to share beautiful stories with children and make a difference in the world."

God was with me, and I improved daily. I attended college, studied animation, and graduated a few years later.

God continues to shine the brightest on my purpose to make a difference in this beautiful world during the darkest times.

Sometimes, life is unpredictable. Be grateful for challenges, they can bring you peace, and you never know, they might be turning points in your life.

Make every effort to keep the unity of the Spirit through the bond of peace.

Ephesians 4:3

A Daily Gift of Peace
by Lucia Murphy

Lately, I've been choosing peace like it's my job. Not because life got quieter, but because I finally stopped letting the noise in.

I used to give so much energy to things that didn't serve me—people who only showed up to drain me, conversations that left me heavy, and online negativity that tried to tell me who I wasn't. But one day, I realized: I don't owe anyone my inner calm or my attention if it costs me my joy.

Now, I protect my peace like it's sacred. I don't engage with drama. I don't match energy—I guard mine. I've started saying no without guilt, and yes to what lifts me: music, food, movement, prayer, creativity, faith, and love.

Stepping away from negative energy isn't always easy. It's tempting to clap back, to explain yourself, to defend your truth. But trust me— *silence and distance* are their own kind of power. Not everyone deserves a response, and not everything deserves your time.

And the best part? My spirit feels lighter. I can hear myself think. I breathe deeper. I feel joy in the little things again—morning coffee, sunshine through the window, a quiet walk, a warm hug, Glynn's laugh in the next room.

Peace isn't the absence of chaos. It's the decision to stay grounded and grateful, no matter what's swirling around you. It's choosing what feeds your soul over what drains it. That's the gift I've given myself— and one I wish for everyone reading this today. Because peace is powerful. And it's yours to claim.

Bracelets Made of Grass
by Katerina Pappas

When I think of *peace,* I think of the song Elton John wrote for Marilyn Monroe upon her passing, *Candle in the Wind.* And yes, I do realize the irony there.

It describes a life marred by turbulence but also a deep inner ability to remain still when it mattered. Because in this life of polarity, everything is experienced in tandem with its opposite.

So, to start, I'd like to remind mostly myself and whoever is reading this that there is no such thing as a good life with only peace. A good life is one with texture, depth, and meaning that derives itself from integrating a degree of chaos.

When I think of *peace,* I am also reminded of a special time I spent with a friend, nearly 10 years ago.

In an attempt to do something "meditative," we decided to go to the nearest park and simply sit on the grass without talking.

We set a timer for ten minutes and just sat there, next to each other, taking in the sounds and sights of the birds and people walking by.

After a few minutes, we both instinctively started to play with the grass, plucking out a couple of blades and braiding them into little bracelets.

The ten-minute mark came and went, but as I sat there in silence, I realized I could never have practiced this type of "peace" with just anyone.

In a way, that simple activity of simply "being together" was the ultimate sign of how much harmony and peace already existed within our friendship.

The nervous system is capable of incredible healing when it experiences peace. That is why they say that true healing can only occur in a state of complete relaxation.

When I think of *peace*, I think of heartbeats that come into resonance with each other, and who beat steadfastly through the winds of life.

The Day Peace Returned

By Mary Vovers Brown

*If we have no peace, it is because we have
forgotten that we belong to each other.*

Mother Teresa

In a quiet village once alive with laughter and unity, something had shifted. Time and trials had worn down the bonds that once connected neighbor to neighbor. The shared meals were gone, replaced by closed doors and cold glances. People passed each other like shadows—present, but distant.

One morning, as the fog clung to the narrow streets, an older woman named Tamina made her way through the square. Her steps were slow, but purposeful. At the market, she saw a young man struggling to lift heavy crates. Without hesitation, she stepped forward and helped him.

He blinked in surprise. "Thank you," he said, catching his breath.

Tamina smiled gently. "I think we've forgotten that we belong to each other."

Something shifted in that moment—something quiet but powerful.

In the days that followed, kindness began to bloom. The young man helped a child reunite with her mother. The mother visited a lonely widow unexpectedly. The widow exchanged smiles and warm words with strangers at the market. Slowly, the village rediscovered what it had lost— not just peace, but the simple truth that we are meant to carry each other.

And so, peace returned—not by force, but by remembering.

The peace of God, which transcends all understanding.

Philippians 4:7

The C.U.P. of Peace
by Mark Heidt

What we've got here... is failure to communicate.
from the movie, *Cool Hand Luke*

Often, a breach of peace between people, even nations, is due to miscommunication, followed by a lack of communication, which leads to discord, litigation, divorce, and even war.

So how do we remedy this, even avoid miscommunication in the first place?

Stephen Covey provides an answer from the book, *7 Habits of Highly Effective People*: Habit 5: Seek First to Understand, Then to Be Understood, which is based on the principle of respect and is about listening before we speak.

My business experience has shown Covey's answer to be true, yet it fails in one respect. That is, it assumes the parties are willing to communicate to begin with in the first place.

Therefore, I followed and encouraged those with whom I had a breach of peace to follow the *C.U.P. rule. Communication leads to Understanding and Peace.*

Once the parties agree to C.U.P. and then Habit Five, the next step is to remind each other of reconciliation and peace; it does not have to be my way, or your way, but a better way, as Henry Boye wrote; *The most important trip you may take in life is meeting people halfway* from the book *Selling Songs Successfully.*

To that end, think in terms of each party having something they want, and to achieve that end, there will have to be some give and take. Remind each other that while we both would like the best outcome for ourselves, the reality is that if the outcome is something we both can live with, it is a good outcome. That is what is called a win/win or no-deal approach, again, Stephen Covey Habit Four: Think win/win.

Daily Gift of Peace
by Pastor Jack Rehill

Isaiah 26:3 says that God will keep in perfect peace those whose mind is stayed on Him, because they trust in him. The word mind has to do with our thinking, our thoughts, intellect, and capacity to understand. The word stayed in Hebrew means to lean on, depend on, fixed on, focused on. The word keep in Hebrew means to guard, preserve, to keep close. The word peace in Hebrew is shalom, meaning welfare, safety, tranquility, rest, the absence of agitation or discord.

When we put it all together, we can say that God will guard, preserve, and keep close in perfect welfare, safety, tranquility, and rest with no agitation or discord, those whose thinking, thoughts, intellect, and capacity to understand, lean on, depend on, or fixed on, and focused on God.

What is the key to all of it? Because they TRUST in Him. No matter what happens, no matter what I'm going through, no matter what I'm facing, I can have the peace that goes beyond the natural understanding and potential consequences of it all because I have complete trust and confidence in the only wise God who is over and above it all.

This is how we can have the daily gift of peace. A gift is not something I've earned. It is something someone else earned and gave to me.

The Lord Jesus says in John 14:27, "Peace I leave with you, My peace I give to you, let not your heart be troubled." I may have heart trouble, job trouble, family trouble, but my heart doesn't have to be troubled because I trust in him.

Let the peace of Christ rule in your hearts.

Colossians 3:15

Peace: Slogans to Live By

by Monica Talbot-Kerkes

Peace. As a recovering alcoholic, I think about the slogans. Slogans that are so simple. Slogans that I often forget. Slogans that can work for everyone, not just an alcoholic like me. Some slogans you may know, others you may not. Maybe they will bring you peace.

Take it Easy:

- When you are in a panic and life feels out of control, just look around and slow down. Almost everything can wait… at least for a minute.

- You are usually running for nothing.

Practice an Attitude of Gratitude:

- Gratitude is the key. Most have so much, compared to so many others. When life seems too much, you must remember all you have. Just look around. And remember.

- Be grateful for what you got, even if it is not a lot.

HALT! Hungry – Angry – Lonely - Tired?

- Which one are you? Are you hungry? Are you lonely? Are you all? If so, you are in trouble. These are physical and emotional triggers for any unhealthy behavior. You need to recognize how you are feeling, so you do not hurt yourself or someone else.

- Pause, then proceed.

One Day at a Time
The most well-known slogan. The most difficult to practice.

- Have no guilt about the past. Those days, you can never get back. Do not worry about the future. These days, you cannot control.
- You can do anything for one moment, one minute, or one day at a time.

Breath in Peace. Breathe out Anxiety.

My publisher told me to do this. It is more a practice than a slogan, but it works. Thanks, Teresa!

A Prayer for Peace

Author Unknown

Loving and Merciful God,
We come before You with hearts longing for peace in our lives,
our families, and our world.
When we are burdened by fear, grant us calm.
When we are divided by anger, show us the way of forgiveness.
When we are surrounded by conflict, help us stand as bearers of
light and hope.

Let peace begin within us—
Shaping our thoughts, guiding our words,
and inspiring our actions.
Bless our homes with harmony, our communities with
understanding, and our nations with unity.
May Your spirit of peace dwell richly in us, so that everywhere we
walk, love is planted, hope is restored,
and peace becomes possible.

In Your Holy Name We Pray,
Amen

The Portal To Peace Lies Within
by Amanda Beth Johnson

Have you ever felt that peace was just beyond your reach—hidden in the spaces between your thoughts, just beyond the daily rush?

Peace, I've learned as an intuitive healer, isn't a far-off destination or a prize for perfect living. It is a quiet current running beneath life's noise—a frequency already alive within your soul, simply waiting to be remembered. Even as the world swirls with demands and distractions, peace exists beneath it all: the steady hum beneath the mind's chatter, the gentle shimmer of light between worries, the truth that calls you home.

Rather than seeking peace somewhere "out there," let's discover it right here, in the present moment. Pause now and breathe deeply. Place your hand on your heart. Notice how your breath softens, how your shoulders release, and how your spirit responds to stillness. Your body already knows the way.

Ask yourself:

- What does peace truly feel like in my body, in my energy?
- What if I let this feeling guide me through my day?

There is a sacred rhythm moving within you. Peace is not a reward for doing more or being perfect—it's a birthright and an inner sanctuary, always available no matter your circumstances.

- You are the magic.
- You are the temple.
- You are the peace you seek.

Let today be the day you pause, breathe, and come home to yourself. Savor this moment with gratitude, and allow your internal peace to ripple outward, touching everything you do.

You are, and always have been, the very portal to your own peace.

*Peacemakers who sow in peace reap
a harvest of righteousness.*

James 3:18

Peace in Pieces

Mary Vovers Brown

Alia stood in the rubble of what was once her childhood home, eyes stinging from dust and memory. A small, single blue tile, cracked but whole, peeked through the ash. She slipped it into her pocket without knowing why.

When Alia arrived in the new country, everything was unfamiliar: the language, the food, even the sky. But the tile remained in her coat pocket, a small reminder of where she had been. At the Community Center, she signed up for an art class. Surrounded by older women, some children, and a few others like her, she was offered a tray of broken tiles. The volunteer explained, "It's Mosaic Day. We create beauty from the broken." She froze. Reaching into her pocket, she extracted the little tile and placed it down as the start of her first creation.

Each week, Alia returned. She learned to fit shattered pieces together, to make patterns from the chaos. Playing with color and texture, she created images of hope. A dove in flight. A home surrounded by a flourishing garden. A butterfly perched on a flower. The Center held an Art Show. People came. They asked questions. Listened. One woman cried.

Alia began teaching others. Refugees, survivors, and war veterans filled the studio. Together, they built benches, murals, and stories. The art didn't erase their pain but held it gently. A journalist asked what their mosaics meant. Alia smiled. "Peace doesn't come whole. It comes in pieces. We just have to choose to put them together." And beneath her fingertips, broken things became something beautiful.

Pearl of Great Price

by Mary Sanford

T he voice on the phone sounded a bit familiar. It was Petra from high school. On a holiday weekend when I was busy, she told my now ex-husband that he and I should get divorced since we were both so unhappy.

She was crying. "I'm so sorry. I shouldn't have interfered in your marriage. Can we meet?" she asked.

We met the following week.

As I do every day, I pray before I leave the house. Frankly, I had nothing to say to Petra, but I knew God would see me through.

Petra brought me flowers, and with tears, she apologized again. You see, unlike me, my husband, Mike, only had two friends: domineering Petra and her husband, Ron. Mike was like an eager puppy: he would've done anything for them.

Me? After the divorce, I turned to the only one I could count on, my Father-Mother God. I knew He'd see me through.

When Petra finished speaking, silence. I listened. Out of nowhere, this angel message came out, a still calm voice, my voice.

"You know, Petra, you did me a great favor. Remember the story of Joseph in the Bible where he's thrown into a pit by his brothers, sold into slavery, and then eventually saves a nation from starvation? He could have given up, but he didn't. What you did was horrible, not only to me but to Mike, who saw you and Ron as his only friends.

God saw me through. If you hadn't caused the divorce, I might not be sitting here today a tenured community college professor, an independent traveler, and happy.

Yes, you did a terrible thing to interfere with another person's marriage. But in the end, this brought me closer to God. And that was a pearl of great price."

Now may the Lord of peace himself
give you peace at all times.

2 Thessalonians 3:16

Desperately Seeking Solace

by Peggy Willms

Have you ever lost a family member, and years later, you are still angry at them? That's me. I can hear all of you whispering advice to me as I write this to you, but it might fall on deaf ears.

I have tried for nearly five years to get over the anger for someone who has passed. I understand that anger only affects the person who holds it, but I still struggle with it. I know the stages of grief and taking baby steps to improve any state of mind. Heck, as a health and wellness coach, I teach it. And rest assured, I am getting close to forgiveness, which will hit anger over the head with a sledgehammer.

You see, I found devastating paperwork stored deep in a closet after a family member passed away that forever changed the half-century of my existence. I was not a product of rape. I was not unwanted. In fact, I was the product of a couple who were very much in love but were unfortunately too young to survive the tolls of raising a family in their teens. After this person's passing, I read document after document that reared up so much emotion that I raced to the backyard to vomit.

After nearly five years, I am working through the anger towards someone who chose to tell me a particular story for my whole life, tainting my beliefs about my existence. Most of us do our best when faced with difficult decisions, but we must find it in our hearts to tell the truth, even if it is difficult, as it can alter the lives of those around us.

As I sit here, I continue to desperately seek solace.

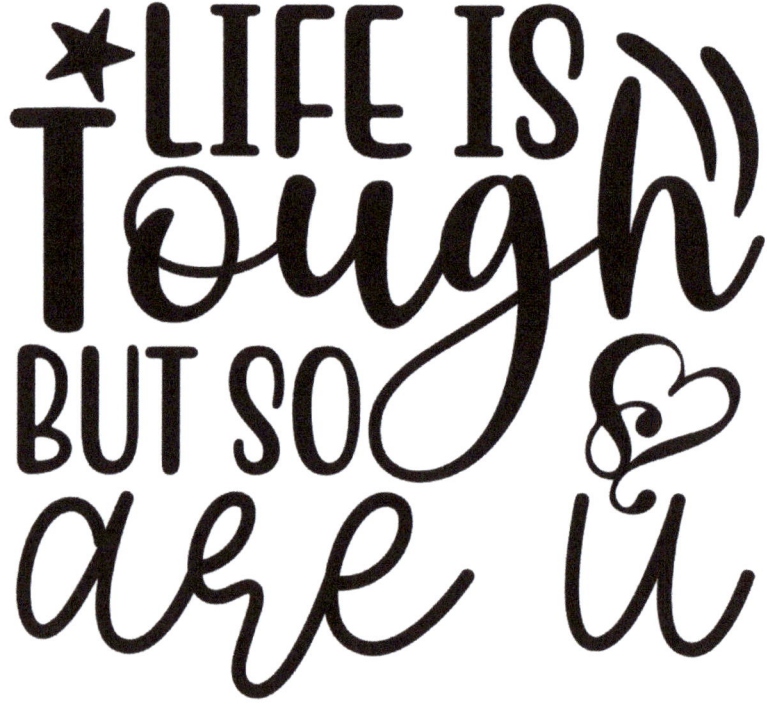

There's No Victory in Being a Victim

by Meredith Woolverton

Identifying as a victim can trap us in persistent anger. Hatred harms us more than those who wronged us, like drinking poison, expecting the other person to die.

Moving toward peace and victory starts by not being a victim. As a child, I was sent on vacation with a family member known for abusing children, which profoundly affected me. My mother's approach was silence, leading to deep insecurities and resentment toward both her and my abuser. Ultimately, forgiving them—without allowing the abuser back into my life—freed me from pain and anger, enabling me to find peace and move forward.

This led to breaking the cycle of abuse in my family. Forgiveness doesn't mean maintaining a close personal relationship with the abuser; however, it does release us to find true peace. This is not a quick fix; it's a process of not allowing myself to be a victim but living in victory.

He himself is our peace.

Ephesians 2:14

Elemental Peace
by Dorchelle Spence

Valleys are universal low places. Shadows of overwhelm, doubt, and fear harbor within their depths. Living in those valleys can be difficult, demeaning, draining. Yet, circumstances may seem to bind us there, providing scant opportunity to leave. But leave we must.

We must–now and then–allow ourselves to explore the other elements of our world. Journey to where the bright sun banishes the shadows, colors in the pallor of doubt, and fuels the blessed assurance of eventual triumph.

Find that place where the air is different. Slightly denser. Tinged with salt. Floating always on a breeze. The kind of air that reminds us to breathe.

Go where the earth too is changed. Softer, smoother, more pliable. Shifting beneath our weight, cushioning the blows. Accepting, then releasing, them, unharmed. Bits–tiny grains of sand–adhering to us, gifts to take back home. Reminders of the respite it gives.

Enter the water that draws our spirit, cleanses our wounds, restores our faith. Allow the moon's tender sway of the ocean to lull away our worries. It's gentle ebb and flow to coax out our anxiety, invite our souls to frolic among its spray. Its waves to wash over us, cover our troubles, drown out the voices of doubt, and imbue us with the sounds of universal peace. Swoosh…Swoosh…Shush…Shush.

May we ever find our way there.

The Rebel, The Crooner, and a Song Across Time

by Mary Vovers Brown

I wasn't going to watch some dusty old Christmas special with Grandpa. Too boring. He had his cocoa, his cardigan, and his ancient TV. I thought about sneaking out. But then, David Bowie was on the TV screen, all elegance and cheekbones, being greeted by crooner, Bing Crosby. I froze. My curiosity was tingling. These two couldn't be more different. When they started singing, I felt something shift. It wasn't about conformity or rebellion anymore. It was about harmony. Generations blending. I felt part of something bigger and leaned against Grandpa's shoulder. Bowie permitted me to be weird, but that night, he also gave me hope. Even rebels want peace.

I was 84 and cranky. My grandson grumbled about watching the Christmas special. I rolled my eyes, but then Bing appeared. Memories cascaded through my mind: radio days, dancing with Lily at the USO, the folly of youth. Bing welcomed in this pale, androgynous-looking fellow, David Bowie. I braced for absurdity. But then, they started to sing. Together. The old world and the new, side by side. My grandson leaned into me as the song played. No words, just a quiet closeness. I felt something I hadn't in years - connected, not by age or taste, but by longing for peace. That moment stitched us together. "Peace on Earth, can it be?"

And the God of peace will be with you.

Philippians 4:9

Daily Gift of Peace

by Gloria Sloan

The concept of the gift of peace is often emphasized, finding peace through faith, surrendering to a higher power, and reconciliation with oneself and others. Yet, I see the gift of peace as an intellectually personal journey, one that brings profound satisfaction to my mind, body, and soul. I'm intrigued by the guidance of peace when it boldly works through my spirit. In a Christian context, the gift of peace is often associated with God's grace and the Holy Spirit. In many spiritual traditions, peace is seen as a gift from God, a blessing bestowed upon individuals in need of seen and unseen things in the world. Beyond anyone's understanding from fleeting circumstances, it's a deep-seated calm amidst trials and tribulations that is a gift to all of us. The gift of peace should not be taken for granted but acknowledged through the powerful practices of meditation, gratitude, mindfulness, and forgiveness.

To expand further into the gifts of peace, nurturing positive relationships plays a crucial role in cultivating and achieving inner peace. This type of peace embraces self-awareness, fosters self-love, and connects with others in a place that brings calmness and understanding. The practical benefit of inner peace is the positive impact it has on mental well-being, building stronger relationships, and boosting self-esteem. It allows individuals to navigate life's challenges with greater resilience and compassion. As a life coach, inner peace is recognized through acceptance, contentment, and being in harmony with yourself, others, and the world around you. It's essential to help facilitate self-discovery that aligns actions with core values, ultimately leading to a more fulfilling life. Peace is a gift that will support you during these challenges and difficulties with a tranquil and accepting mind.

The Empowering Comfort of Peace
by Johnny Tan

My journey in discovering the empowering comfort of peace is an endearing one. I can still remember that Saturday morning when I received a phone call from my sister in Malaysia at 6 am. She told me our mom is in the ICU and she will not make it past the next 24 hours.

Since I live in the US, I told her I would be home by Wednesday and to let our mom know. I was in tears all weekend long. Then everything changed when I boarded the plane on Monday. I sensed that my mom would hang on for me. My energy changed. I was at the hospital beside my mom on Wednesday, feeling calm and collected.

The calmness continued as I kissed my mom's forehead, stroking her hair, and whispering to her, "Nyah, it is OK, I am here, it is time to go, and we love you," as she lay peacefully in her bed at home. Everyone else was crying; however, I was empowered with the unique energy of peace. My mom had shared with me years ago that regardless of who we are, whether we are a king or a beggar, when we take our last breath, we are all the same.

As my mom took her last breath to transit this world, I sensed peace within. I felt empowered with a never-before-felt spiritual grace of the heart, mind, body, and spirit. My sister and our relatives were crying loudly, expressing their feelings of sadness.

This lasting experience with my mom 12 years ago forever changed my perspective about life and death. To this day, I still possess within me the empowering comfort of peace!

Make every effort to live in peace with everyone.

Hebrews 12:14

Look Up and Listen

by Joyce Waring

"You keep him in perfect peace whose mind is stayed on you, because he trusts in you." Isaiah 26:3 ESV

So many places in my life are passages, pathways to peace. I will share a few, in hopes that one of them will resonate with you as well.

There are those times I am the first one to wake and walk through the silent house, fix my morning cup of hot tea, and sit expectantly in my snuggly chair with God's Word open in my lap. PEACE.

Living in the country, I am privy to hearing the frogs making their evening music in the pond and the bevy of quail that live in the spruce tree singing their goodnight song. PEACE.

Walking along the river, breathing in all its beauty, I hear the rush of water drowning out all my noisy thoughts. PEACE.

Sometimes when the wind blows in the late afternoon, I catch the clang and bang of the giant windchime and with it the more delicate sound of the tiny chime, reminding me that though the wind blows where it will, in my life, I can endure and respond in beauty. PEACE.

An old wooden swing perched above the cliffs of the Deschutes River beckons me just to sit. Gentle breezes ruffle my hair and skim my face as I focus on the soft, fluffy clouds above the rugged rock face of the canyon below. PEACE.

What is the common denominator here? It is God and His creation. Seek your PEACE in Him. He is waiting for you and does not disappoint.

The Quiet Between Waves

by Mary Vovers Brown

T he sun hadn't yet touched the water. I sat straddling my board, rocking gently, waiting for the next set. Around me, the ocean breathed in hushes and sighs, a lullaby only the early risers heard. It had been a month since Mom passed. Everyone said the same things: "She's in a better place," "Time will heal," "You have to stay strong." But none of that made sense out here, where time was marked by swell and sky, and strength meant letting go, not holding on.

A wave rolled beneath me, low and lazy. I didn't chase it. I just floated, eyes closed, breath steady. In that moment, there was nothing. No noise, no push, no grief. Just the stillness between things. And that's when I heard her. Not her voice exactly, but her presence. In the quiet. Just like she used to wake me before dawn, whispering, "Let's catch the sunrise." No advice. No sadness. Just being. With me.

I opened my eyes. The sea glittered. Another set was rising in the distance. I paddled forward, not to escape the pain, but because I could. I caught the wave. For six, maybe seven seconds, I danced across the water. It didn't last. Peaceful moments, like this one, never do. Not forever.

But as I walked up the beach, board underarm, I smiled. The wave was gone. The peace remained, like salt on skin, a constant reminder that healing is possible.

Blessed are the peacemakers.

Matthew 5:9

Hot or Cold

by Linette Rainville

*The Lord says, 'I will guide you along the best pathway
for your life. I will advise you and watch over you*
Psalm 32:8 (NLT)

When I was young, hanging out with my cousins, one of our favorite games was *Hot or Cold*. One of us would hide an object, and the rest of us had to find it. The hider would shout clues like, "Hot, hot—you're getting close!" or "Cold—brrr, you're way off!" We'd laugh and cheer as the finder got warmer or colder with every step.

Funny enough, that simple game taught me something about finding God's peace.

These days, when I'm facing a big decision or seeking direction, I always start with prayer. But then, I move. I take a step toward something and pay close attention to what I feel in my spirit.

Sometimes I head down a path that might look great on the outside— but if I start to feel my peace slipping away, I've learned to pause. That's often my cue to take a step back.

And then there are other times. The path might be hard or stretching me, but as I walk, there's a steady warmth, a quiet knowing. That's His peace. It's like hearing that inner *"hot, hot, hot!"*—the Holy Spirit gently guiding me forward.

You've probably heard the phrase: *No Jesus, no peace.*

Know Jesus, KNOW PEACE.

It's true. Life offers us many choices—plenty that may look good on the outside.

But only one path is the best one: the one that brings lasting peace, the one Jesus has marked out for us.

And friend, that peace? It's worth following every time.

trust THE TIMING of your LIFE

Inner Sanctuary

by Eileen Bild

When I think of peace, I feel a deep sense of well-being that touches my mind, body, and spirit. But as a young stay-at-home mom raising four children, peace felt out of reach. Life was constant motion—meeting everyone's needs but my own.

In my mid-30s, my health collapsed under the pressure. That breaking point pushed me inward, initiating a powerful journey of self-discovery. I realized I had been giving endlessly without ever replenishing myself. Meditation and mindfulness became my lifeline—anchors in the storm. I learned to shut out the noise, embrace stillness, and reconnect with my inner self.

In meditation, I found a sacred inner sanctuary—a tranquil waterfall, a quiet bench—where I could just be. Each visit left me lighter, clearer, and deeply at peace.

Though the world is full of noise and chaos, we each have the power to return to stillness. Even a moment of mindful breathing can shift everything. Peace must be nurtured and honored. Place your hands over your heart, sit in stillness, and let that become the spark that shapes your life.

They must seek peace and pursue it.

1 Peter 3:11

Finding Peace Through Turmoil
by Patricia Giankas

Two years ago, life brought me to my knees.

After more than 20 years building a company from the ground up, I fell ill—without clear answers or diagnosis. I had to step back. And when I did, the company I had poured my soul into moved on without me. No "thank you." No compensation. Just silence.

Around the same time, I helped a U.S. company—led by someone with a checkered past—expand to Canada and secure a major deal. On the very day that deal launched, I received a cease-and-desist letter. From people I had only ever helped. Again, no "thanks." No payment. Just betrayal. My heart broke. And worse—my spirit cracked.

Then came the waves: my father fell ill and passed, my mother, now living with advanced dementia, entered long-term care, and my husband was diagnosed with stage four Parkinson's. I cashed in every RRSP, every bond—everything—just to survive. I am 70+ and starting over.

With prayer as my only constant, I began again. Rebuilding the dream—the app—I once hoped would lift others. It's taken far longer than planned. Most days, I had no funding, no strength, and no safety net. I often asked, "Why me, God?" Now I see I was being refined for something greater.

Though I've lost almost everything—my company, my finances, my old life—I have gained something deeper: Wisdom. Compassion. Unshakable faith. But I was never alone.

I am surrounded by amazing people—especially my night school friends of 52 years. And God has sent angels, time and again, to help me through these trying times.

The companies I helped are thriving. They never looked back. But I have chosen to look forward—with purpose. Peace didn't come from fighting. It came from surrendering to what I could not control—and trusting what I still could create.

I am still here. Still building. Still believing.

INNER PEACE
is the new
SUCCESS

A Fine Line Between Helping and Enabling
Meredith Woolverton

For several years, my daughter, Sandra, experienced challenges related to drug addiction. As her mother, I also faced decisions about which actions supported or hindered her recovery. Shortly before Thanksgiving, I received a phone call informing me that she had been arrested. I decided not to bail her out of jail. She strongly disagreed with this choice. The intention behind my decision was to allow her to take responsibility for her actions, which included refraining from providing financial support. There is a balance required because individuals in recovery benefit from support.

Choosing not to provide financial assistance can be difficult for a parent. However, it allowed me to feel assured that I was not contributing financially if an overdose occurred. This helped me accept that it is possible to offer support without interfering with the recovery process.

Recovery is an individual process requiring personal commitment. It tends to be more effective when the person in recovery is internally motivated rather than doing it for others. Initially, recovery may involve self-focus, and after progress is made, family members can become involved. My experience of setting boundaries allowed me to avoid enabling and find peace.

We currently maintain a positive and healthy relationship. I am proud of the steps Sandra has taken in her recovery and her commitment to her sobriety every day. As a family, we all battled our own addictions and have overcome them together. Mine was alcohol, my husband was gambling, and it's all the same recovery process.

Eye of the Storm

by Tammy Hader

D ad sits on the edge of the hospice bed set up in his and Mom's bedroom and whips his head side to side until his focus stops on the wall in front of him. He mumbles a warning about someone in a doorway on the bedroom wall. I glance at the empty space, just in case. I see no one there. The morphine the hospice worker told me to administer kicks in, Dad lies down, and I wish for a distraction.

I look up to see Tabbey, his reclusive cat, sitting in the doorway. Typically, she cowers under the sofa, hiding her green eyes and grey stripes. Today, she studies Dad with solemn interest. I flinch when she lifts her head and locks eyes with me. An omen isn't exactly what I had in mind.

Dad calls out to his grandson, severing my connection with Tabbey. Entrenched in other priorities miles away, Dad's grandchildren live in blissful ignorance of his delirium.

"Wesley's in the bathroom," I lie to calm him and steal a quick glance at the doorway.

Tabbey has vanished, like a dream erased by awakening eyelids. That's when I hear it – the death rattle – the struggle to stay alive as the body drowns in death. No one told me this was happening today, except Tabbey.

And then, stillness. I inhale a gasp of panic right before an eerie undertow pulls a wave of tranquility through the room and relaxes me into a tearless calm. Dad's lifeless body and I rest at peace in the eye of the storm. No one else knows it's over … just us.

The fruit of the Spirit is love, joy, peace.

Galatians 5:22

Go Fish

by Anne O'Brien

"Come on, hop in the truck. The fisherman should be in soon," Dad sang. Down went the clutch. Dad shoved the truck into first gear, and off we went, laughing and chatting all the way to the Connecticut River.

It was Connecticut River Shad season. And when you own a fish market, as my dad did, you're excited about getting the freshest catch.

The sun shone in all her glory, with hues of orange and red, fighting to stay up for one moment longer. She waited for us for us to reach the river.

I felt the dampness of the river air. It held the diesel fumes from the boats that twirled around my little legs. It was getting cool, and mosquitoes were waking up. But I didn't care. What six-year-old gets to hang out by the river with the big guys and her dad?

Escorted by the setting the sun, the boats rolled in slowly so as not to cause a wake. The tired fishermen were proud of the bounty they delivered.

I don't know what was most beautiful about that trip. Was it the sun's dance over the river with her rays waltzing over the waves? Could it have been the cicadas, providing rhythm for the sun's dance? Was it my father's face, lit with smiles and kinship for the fishermen? Or was it my love for my dad and his love for me?

I know it was all those things, those simple pleasures of life, that are gone after the first glimpse. That's what the child in me savors. The gift of the glimpse and its peaceful rhythms give me ballast to carry on.

Whenever I feel lost, I know where I'll go: I'll go fish.

Finding Peace Through the Dance of Addiction

Michelle Rene' Hammer

When we were little girls on family road trips, my sister and I made peace signs out the car window. We huddled together in the back seat, afraid while going over bridges. We pulled "make-believe" air horns while passing large trucks, giggling gleefully when truckers honked back. We thought we were so cool!

Only 18 months apart, we were each other's first, best friends. We chased lightning bugs, caught butterflies, and learned to swim together. We made animal sounds at bedtime, played childhood games, rode bikes, skinned knees, made snow angels, and did a zillion other things together. We would fight and make up, but we ALWAYS had each other's backs.

That all changed when addiction took charge. Hers, Dad's, and other family members who abused alcohol. Nothing was the same— no more late-night sharing, fighting, and making up, or play dates with our kids. Giggles, "so cool," and having each other's backs became strained words, guarded hearts, and silence. Addiction tore our family apart. Once best friends became strangers. After 40 years of struggling, I finally said NO MORE. And today there is no more us! Not without professional help as recommended, and we all needed it desperately. Addiction treatment isn't just for the person with an addiction. It's for the whole family. The longer the addiction remains, the more the pain grows for everyone. I have lived it firsthand.

When addiction is in charge, the family takes on roles: Addict & Enabler, Hero & Scapegoat, Lost Child & Mascot, helping addiction continue. Each person plays their part and knows their steps in this complicated, painful dance, until finally, someone doesn't, and without a warning, the dance stops. Now what, you ask? For some families, everyone fights to keep it together, all seeking treatment, and the family recovers.

For many families, that's not the case. But the dance of addiction stops for the person who says no more. Those people come out of it alive. Alive is good. Alive is free. Free to stop playing a role and become who GOD intended you to be. I know. Because it's happened to me. After ten years of recovery from the painful dance of addiction, my life is so much more peaceful and fully alive!

What happens to the addict? That's an excellent question that people are afraid to answer or ask. The truth is, every addict is on death row. Their hope is in choosing recovery. You can't save them, but by setting limits, the hope is that they see they are continuing to lose. They are losing to addiction. They are losing time, relationships, and many other things. The hope is that they stop losing. The hope is that they want something more than what they are addicted to. But it is still their choice, and at least, you are coming out alive!

For me, this is where God comes in. It's too late for my dad, who died when I was a teenager. I pray for my sister. I put her and my hope in God's hands. For me, there is no better place for her or my hope to be — in God's hands — His peace-filled, loving hands.

Note:

If you want recovery today, please reach out. SAMHSA is an excellent resource for persons in crisis, 24 hours a day, 7 days a week. Help is only a prayer and a phone call away. Dial 1-800-662-HELP. You'll never regret it. There is always help and always hope!

Meanwhile, I leave you with this…

What you see isn't all there is.

In Jeremiah 1:5, God says, "Before I formed you in the womb I knew you, before you were born, I set you apart…". and again in Jeremiah, 29.11 God says, "For I know the plans I have for you, declares the Lord, plans to prosper you and not to harm you, plans to give you hope and a future."

God sees and God cares.

Lean into His peaceful arms and decide whether you want his plans or not, just as it's up to the person with an addiction to decide if now is the time for recovery.

Being Peace Is The Only Path To Peace
by Carla Lee Johnston

Peace, in its most profound sense, is not a passive prayer whispered into the wind. It is not born from thought or conjured by chants in meditation.

Peace is a living lifeforce—an embodiment of love expressed, an unwavering alignment with *The Divine* essence within. It is not the absence of conflict, but the radiant presence of God, breathing through your *Being* and our shared experience.

The world doesn't need another plea for peace. It needs those willing to *be* peace—to *know it and walking its emanation within every breath, within* every word, every silence, every encounter.

To wish for peace without *being* peace is like asking the sun to rise while hiding its light.

True peace begins within—in the sacred pause between stimulus and response, where we choose compassion over judgment, as love's presence over reaction.

The ego's masquerade—within churches, governments, even spiritual circles—dissolves when peace becomes embodiment, not performance.

Every tool we need to end war lives within us now. Dr. Marshall Rosenberg's *Language of Compassion,* rooted in Gandhi's non-violence, is a superpower of love in action.

Unshakeable peace is not earned. *It is remembered.* **It is who we already are beyond our shared wounds of separation.**

The greatest (r)evolution begins by removing the seeds of judgment where they first took root—within the belief we are separate.

Today, in every choice, create the sacred *"gap"* where your heart abides as peace.

Not as future hope, but as the living *Truth* of who you are.

Breathe.

Choose peace within the *I AM* **emanating presence.**

That sets our world free.

An excerpt from The Book: *Unveiling The Truth, The Journey Within* available at: www.thetruthjourney.com

---

Another Prayer for Peace in the World
Author Unknown

God, we pray for the power to be gentle,
the strength to be forgiving,
the patience to be understanding,
and the endurance to accept the consequences
of holding to what we believe to be right.

May we put our trust in the power of good to overcome evil
and the power of love to overcome hatred.

We pray for the vision to see and the faith to believe
in a world emancipated from violence,
a new world where fear shall no longer lead us to
commit injustice, nor selfishness make us
bring suffering to others.

Help us to devote our lives and thoughts,
and energy to the task of making peace,
praying always for the inspiration and
the power to fulfill the destiny
for which we were all created.

On earth peace to men on whom his favor rests.

Luke 2:14

Peace in Black and White
by Mark O'Brien

This story reminds me that gifts of kindness can also be gifts of peace.

In October of my 20th year (1974), I took a job driving a truck for a construction company.

On Christmas Eve morning that year, I delivered materials in New Haven, Connecticut. It snowed heavily. Heading out of town, I noticed two African-American women standing alongside a car on the right side of the street. The rear tire on the driver's side was flat. I stopped.

I said, "Good morning, ladies. Do you need help?" They smiled and said they did. I asked if they had a jack and a spare tire. They said they did. I asked if they'd like to get back in their car and stay warm. They said they would.

I said, "If you'll open the trunk first, I'll take care of the rest." They did. And I did.

After changing the tire, I walked to the driver's window, knocked, and told the ladies I was finished. They got out of the car.

The passenger approached me with cash in her hand. She said, "Please let us pay you for helping us."

I said, "Thank you. That's very thoughtful. But I'm not comfortable taking your money."

They asked in unison, "Why?"

"If I'd been the one in need and you stopped to help me, would you expect to be paid?"

They replied, "No!"

"There you go. I knew that."

They asked if they could repay me in some way.

I said, "Yes. You can do me a favor."

They said they'd be happy to.

I said, "Please tell your friends Santa's a skinny white dude."

They laughed. I hugged both of them. And we went our respective ways with peace in our very full hearts.

The Calm After the Storm

By Peggy Willms

It was September 28, 2022, and Hurricane Ian was headed directly at us. Yes, I live in Florida. Yes, we chose not to evacuate. And for nine hours, we hunkered down without power and water as we ran around the house with large bins, capturing all the water leaking through the roof and walls.

"After the first half of the eye of the storm passes, the cloud will part, the blue skies will reveal themselves, the birds will sing, and the neighbors will race out to walk their dogs. The speed of this storm, you will have about 45 minutes before the eye circles back counterclockwise and hits you again, so make sure you get back under shelter." Those were the last words spoken by the local weatherman before our power went out.

And he was right.

As Mother Nature's whistling anger diminished, children began screeching, and neighbors peered out their windows. We joined in the quick property assessment party, made sure everyone was ok, and like clockwork, peace and quiet... silence. Though it didn't last long, it reminded me of the turbulence we all face daily.

Maybe there are times in your life when you swirl with change, sorrow, or even trauma. Gently remind yourself that eventually the storm shall pass and the dust will settle. You may not be stuck in the middle of a 156 m.p.h. Hurricane, but peace shall find you even if only for a few minutes. Relish in the calm. Restore. Refresh. And Rebuild

Don't
OVERTHINK IT

God's Peace Perceptual

by Donna Guary

*Peace I leave with you; my peace I give to you.
Not as the world gives do I give to you. Let not your hearts be
troubled, neither let them be afraid.*
John 14:27 (ESV)

Each day we wake up is a fresh gift from God and tucked within that gift is something the world cannot offer: His perfect peace. Jesus, the Prince of Peace (Isaiah 9:6), did not promise us a life without trials. He said we would have trouble (John 16:33). But take heart; He overcame the world.

His peace doesn't fade when the bills stack up, the diagnosis comes, or the loved one drifts away. Instead, it anchors us, reminding us that God is with us, fighting for us, and holding us together even when everything else feels like it's falling apart.

Philippians 4:7 tells us that God's peace "transcends all understanding." It calms the anxious heart and silences the noise of fear. It's not the kind of peace we can earn or figure out; it's a gift, freely given through Christ. It yours.

Today, quiet your heart, fix your mind on God, and trust him, and he will keep you in perfect peace. (Isaiah 26:3) Breathe in His promises. Let His Word renew your mind and His Spirit steady your soul.

The world's peace is temporary and shallow. But God's peace is eternal, deep, and sustaining. It is yours, today and every day.

Prayer: Lord Jesus, thank You for the gift of Your peace. Remind us today to rest in You, no matter what we face. Amen.

The LORD blesses his people with peace.

Psalm 29:11

Finding Inner Peace
by Jen Reed

Sometimes in life, you can come to a point where you are at your lowest and feel like there is no light left in this world. You may have things in your life that you know are important, that matter, and you love in your heart, but your soul is just lost. Every day is a struggle just to climb out of bed, you just go through the motions of life, feeling there is no point or meaning to life. Then one day, someone comes into your life and changes everything, bringing the light back. At first, it is dim like a candle in a dark room, then with time, it grows bigger and brighter and lights up everything and shuts out the darkness.

Their presence in your life seems to make life worth living, you can breathe easier, smile bigger, and laugh louder than ever before. The you that was gone and forgotten has been reborn and reminded of how special your thoughts, feelings, and ideas are. They encourage you to do things you never thought possible, make you feel complete, yet you still have the desire to strive for more. This presence in your life makes you the best version of yourself you never knew was there.

The crazy thing is they never realize what they have done. They don't see the light they radiate into the world. To them, they are just living life being themselves, not doing anything special even though they are. With words, a look, a touch of the hand, or a warm embrace, they make you feel like you can soar to new depths every day and find inner peace.

Peace
On
Earth

Worry Not

by Laurie Rowland

When I was 22, I wrote a poem called *Worry Not*. The irony, I'd been a worrier from the start; afraid of spiders, water, thunderstorms, and the boogie man. Fear and anxiety are worry's two sisters; phantoms, anticipating the next potential or perceived problem. The poem was written as a letter from God, reminding the reader to cast their care upon Him. What I learned during that time and had to continue cultivating was finding and keeping peace: mind, body, and spirit. I had an epiphany. While worry impacts our psyche, health, and relationships, it's powerless to change situations or produce a positive outcome. It's worthless. My source of peace is God.

And the peace of God, which passeth all understanding, shall keep your hearts and minds through Christ Jesus. (Philippians 4:7 KJV)

WORRY NOT

Worry not, my little one; upon me cast all care.
Let not one thing trouble you. Your burdens I will bear.
I lead captives in my train. I set the prisoner free.
All my children are bound in chains, but lo, I hold the key.
Tenderly, I call to you; I touch your fretted brow.
I can work all things for good, just let me show you how.
Learn to trust in me alone. With me, you cannot fail.
Step by step, I help you up the rough and rugged trail.
Worry not, my little one. Let me see you smile.
Realize that I AM God, and rest in me a while.

You will keep in perfect peace those
whose minds are steadfast.

Isaiah 26:3

Peace is a Piece of Cake
by Kathleen (Kat) O'Keefe-Kanavos

Better than a thousand hollow words is one word that brings peace.
Buddha

John Lennon sang, "Give Peace a Chance!" And we sang with him. We hear that we must seek peace for a better life, world, and Universe. But how can we do more than sing about it? If it were easy to give peace a chance, wouldn't we all be doing it?

Perhaps we're thinking too hard, and not "Being" enough. Being loving, thoughtful, and nonjudgmental are the fundamentals of peace. Like love, Peace is less action and more emotion.

To give peace a chance, we must give love a chance.

Love family, friends, and total strangers, as you would have them love you. You may be thinking, *So-and-so is such a pain in the bu**!. I've tried but....* Shhh! "Judge not, that you be not judged."

You don't have to judge everything everyone does to love them unconditionally, just as they don't have to love everything you say or do. Hopefully, that realization just gave you Peace of Mind.

Realizing you don't have to embrace everyone's beliefs to coexist with them in peace is a big step toward achieving World Peace. It makes peace a piece of harmonious cake.

Being a small piece of peace begins at home and is a big step toward World Peace.

The first step is always the hardest. But remember, the great ocean began as one tiny raindrop at a time. Be a raindrop in the Ocean of Peace. Be a ripple of love that kisses distant shores and gives peace a chance.

Peace in the Midst of the Storm

by Renea Attaway

Have you ever been out on a boat, offshore, and far from land? Out there, a storm can rise in minutes. The wind and waves toss you around like you're nothing. In the vastness of the ocean, you realize just how small and powerless you truly are. It's unbelievably frightening—you have no control and are completely at the mercy of nature.

I don't consider myself someone who easily gives in to fear, but I can assure you, when you're on a boat and lightning is cracking, waves are crashing over the sides, rain is pouring down, and the wind is howling as the boat rocks violently—it's terrifying.

There's a story in Mark 4:35–41 about the disciples caught in a storm at sea. Jesus was asleep in the boat, and the disciples cried out, "Master, don't You care that we are perishing?" In verse 39, the Bible tells us that Jesus arose, rebuked the wind, and said to the sea, "Peace, be still!" Instantly, the storm was calmed. All He had to do was speak.

We all face storms in life. They may come in the form of sickness, grief, financial pressure, family troubles, divorce, or abuse. These are just a few of life's storms. But no matter how fierce they are, Jesus is Lord over every storm.

Keep your mind focused on the Prince of Peace and trust in Him.

You will keep him in perfect peace, whose mind is stayed on
You, because he trusts in You.
Isaiah 26:3
In Him, you can always find perfect peace in the midst of the storm.
Shalom

*Inherit the land and delight themselves
in the abundance of peace.*

Psalm 37:11

The Eagle and the Crow
Original Author Unknown

The only bird that dares to attack an eagle is a crow, but the eagle never fights back. Here is why:

1. The crow is the only bird bold enough to sit on the eagle's back and peck at its neck. Relentless. Annoying. But the eagle stays calm.

2. The eagle doesn't flap. Doesn't fight. Doesn't waste energy. It does one thing: It rises.

3. The higher the eagle soars, the thinner the air becomes. The crow? It can't handle the altitude.

4. Eventually, the crow gasps, loses strength, and falls off. Not because the eagle attacked, but because the eagle ascended.

5. Let the crows talk. Let them peck. You don't have to respond. Just keep going higher.

6. They can't follow you forever. Your growth will suffocate their noise.

So don't engage. Elevate!

This story is an excellent example of being true to who you are, using your God given gifts can keep you in a state of peace even when the world is doing its best to distract or even hurt you.

Stay in peace and rise above!

Teresa

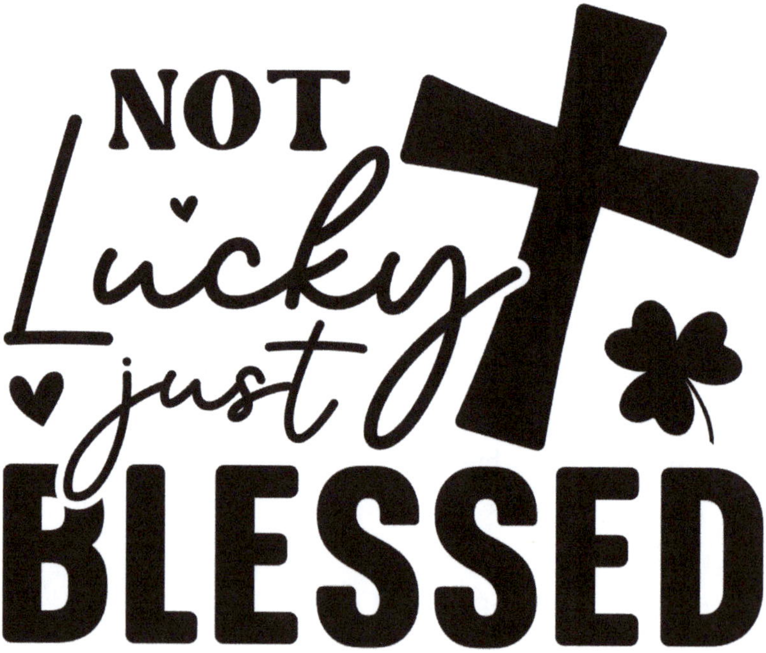
NOT
Lucky
just
BLESSED

Blessed Beyond Measure

by Marla Hamann

I have four beautiful children whom I love with all my heart. My family is my everything. My husband didn't have children of his own, while I had two older boys. When we tried to conceive together, I lost two babies. The grief was overwhelming, and I felt like a failure—as a woman and as a wife. I was ready to give up.

But my husband reminded me of what mattered most: he loved me for me. If children never came, it was okay—we would still be okay, because what he wanted most was me. It took time for that truth to sink in, but when it did, I found peace and focused on being the best me I could be.

Then, by God's grace, we became pregnant. Our daughter, Emma Layne, was born, and I felt complete—two older boys and now a precious baby girl. But life had another surprise. I became pregnant again, and this time we welcomed a little boy. I believe God gave him to us as Emma's protector.

Emma has a disability, but it does not define her. She radiates love, strength, and determination. And though her older brothers have their own lives now, her younger brother, RD (short for Roy Dell IV), is her constant companion and best friend.

A priest once told me that the Bible says, "Love your spouse, and if you lose a child, God will grant you another." That isn't Scripture, and no child could ever replace the ones I lost. But those words gave me a spark of hope.

The moment my husband assured me he wanted us, no matter what, I surrendered to God's plan. Then God blessed us with not one, but two beautiful children, expanding the circle of love in our family.

And the peace of God, which passeth all
understanding, shall keep your hearts and min
Now may the Lord of peace himself
give you peace at all times.

2 Thessalonians 3:16

Jesus, My Peace In The Storm

by Maria Crane

Peace! Be still! And the wind ceased,
and there was a great calm.
Mark 4:39

We all have storms in our lives that need to be calmed. They are an inevitable part of life. My most recent storm came last year when a Christian man, whom we trusted to manage our retirement investments, frauded us out of our lifetime savings. We were devastated by this friend's extreme betrayal and discovered that he was running a Ponzi scheme to finance his extravagant lifestyle with our money. Despite some sleepless nights, I felt the Lord's presence and His gentle reminder: "Be still and know that I am God. Trust me, Maria!"

Our printed money says, "In God we trust," but having our source of income removed revealed my dependence on the dollars we had earned and saved over 4 decades, and made me ask: what do I place my trust in?

My peace was restored consistently when I declared Jesus as my source of peace and spoke His scriptural promises:

"I will keep you in perfect peace, Maria, as your mind is steadfast, because you trust in me." (Isaiah 26:3 NIV)

Maria, I will supply all your needs according to my glorious riches in Christ Jesus. (Phil 4:19 NIV)

Jesus is aware of every trial and storm that I face and allows them to build His character in me. When I am tempted to be anxious about my future, His word anchors my soul in His peace. Then, as I gratefully surrender my circumstances to Him each day, He fills me with great calm.

Peace

by Beth Johnston

D oes a day go by without hearing, thinking or speaking the word peace? News stories, messages among family and friends, the unconscious yet loud thoughts of peace, or the lack thereof, seem to be a part of everyday life these days.

The desire for peace is noble, necessary…naïve?

How will we recognize it if or when it may appear?

Peace is a goal, a worthy one at that. It is the thought or feeling at any moment that makes us feel good about who we are and where we are.

It is where we find it and where we leave it for others.

Peace provides the comfort to close our eyes at night to refresh for another shot at it with each new sunrise.

Peace is a wish we share, even with strangers: "Peace be with you", "May he Rest in Peace", "…and World Peace" are familiar phrases. They are powerful and benevolent.

So, why does peace seem so elusive? Why does one war seem to start the moment 'peace' is declared among other nations? Why does heartache find its way into families where it seems peace should be obvious?

Are we looking for peace, as we do for love, in all the wrong places?

Peace comes from within. Perhaps it is self-indulgent, a state-of-mind & being that makes every single moment acceptable just as it is. It's 'being' good with and about yourself. It's personal calm amid an otherwise chaotic world.

Peace awaits…go find it, go create it and spread it around.

Peace Be With You, today and in every way.

Seek peace and pursue it.

Psalm 34:14

Peaceful Journey

by Carolyn Ballenger

I see so many people walking around with a scowl on their face.
Is this really the fate of the whole human race?
It's hard to believe we'll allow ourselves to go out like this.
Reacting from fear and anger rather than living in the bliss.

And if you could just feel in your heart the connection we share.
It would make all these painful encounters so much easier to bear.
When I see Spirit in your eyes and feel it in my heart.
Then our long and peaceful journey is off to a start.

When we change our perspective and see only the best
When we quit working so hard and take time to rest.
When we choose to see Spirit in each living soul
We'll all be that much closer to the goal.

Of sharing our resources so that no one goes without,
Of honoring compassion and creativity, rather than money and clout.
Of healing the wounds that have festered for so long
To create a planet that's peaceful and strong.

Peace Remembered

by Joannie Strickler

The most peaceful time I can remember is when I was little on my me maw's farm rocking back and forth on the porch swing, watching the tall trees sway gently to and fro in the summer breeze, inhaling the sweet smell of honeysuckle, while we snapped green beans to can.

Those days of perfect calm and peace are where I go in my head when this crazy world gets too loud for me, when I need to see past the noise of hard times and remember what matters the most in this life.

It's the journey and memories we make with the people we love. That's the best gift she ever gave me, that knowledge, that heavenly stillness, and those sweet, sweet memories of her loving me. The PEACE she gave me with her calm presence, is what I try to pass down to my children.

Prince of Peace.
Isaiah 9:6

Finding Peace in the Uncertainty
by Lindi Martin

There was a time I couldn't breathe under the weight of it all. The diagnoses, the endless appointments, the cold, sterile rooms where doctors spoke in terms that felt more like warnings than guidance. I'd drive home in silence, my hands clenched on the steering wheel, wondering how I was supposed to survive this version of motherhood.

But peace found me—not all at once, but in quiet moments. In the soft rise and fall of my child's chest after a long day. In the knowing glance between me and a therapist who understands without words. In celebrating tiny milestones that most parents never think to cheer for.

Peace didn't erase the hard. It walked with me through it. On days when the bad news stacks higher than the good, peace reminds me to stay present. When the trauma creeps in—flashing images of hospital beds and beeping monitors—I've learned to breathe through it, to reclaim that moment for myself instead of letting it claim me.

Appointments still fill our calendar. Therapies still ask for everything. But I no longer fight the life we live. I've made peace with the unknown, and in doing so, I've made room for joy to coexist with pain.

I've stopped waiting for normal. This is our normal. And somehow, it's beautiful. Because it's built on a fierce kind of love—the kind that's stitched together with resilience and rest, with tears and laughter, with faith that even in the hardest moments, I am the mother my child needs.

And that truth is my peace.

I Made Peace

by Morgan Danielle

For years, I was consumed by my own chaos.
An anxious mind, a guarded heart, and a body that never felt safe.

I didn't realize it then, but the turmoil I carried was shaping everything around me…Especially my relationships.

The partners I chose were mirrors of the war I was fighting within.
Emotionally unavailable. Abusive. Hot and cold.
Always leaving me questioning my worth.

I thought they were the problem…But they were just reflecting the parts of me I was rejecting.
The ones I tried to hide and felt ashamed of.
The parts I believed made me unlovable.

Everything began to shift when I stopped running from those parts…
And started making peace with them.

When I stopped abandoning my own needs just to feel chosen.
When I stopped labeling myself as "too much" or "not enough."
When I stopped performing, fixing, or proving to earn love.

That's when the battle within me ended.
That's when I finally felt at ease in my body, mind, and life.

The more I loved the pieces I once rejected, the more peace I created.
It started within, then everything around me began to rise to meet me.

Now, I'm loved by a man who honors my heart.
Who doesn't want to change me.
Who brings calm instead of confusion.

Because I'm no longer addicted to chaos.
No longer available for anything that disturbs my peace.

And it all began the moment I made peace with myself.

To guide our feet into the path of peace.

Luke 1:79

Everything I Need

by Dr. Anne Worth

You already have everything you need!
1 Corinthians 3:16b (Passion Translation)

When I read this scripture, I thought, *I have everything?* And then, I asked a different question: *"I have everything I need to do what?"* I'm not going to run a marathon at 82. I'm not going to end a war, although I can pray about ending it. I'm not going to turn back the clock.

Every person would answer this question differently. I think it is a good question to ask ourselves. And how you answer that question will reveal something perhaps you haven't thought about.

I asked some folks to show how they would answer, and here are a few results that were shared with me:

I have everything I need to graduate.

I have everything I need to be a good mother.

I have everything I need to write a book.

My answer is not about a worldly accomplishment.

My answer is about the deepest desire of my life: I have everything I need to be at peace…because God gave me this gift

And He wants to give this grace and peace to everyone.

Peace In The Storm

by Kate Rohauer

Everyone faces storms, but some are catastrophic. Our family was devastated in 1998 with the murder of my youngest daughter, Lynette. There are few words to describe the turmoil and devastation that it caused.

Many people think that once the trial is over and the perpetrator is convicted and sentenced for life, the family should go on, case closed. I wish it were that simple. Unless you personally experience the justice system, the lies, and the division of families, you can't begin to understand the tempests that can blow in and turn your world upside down again. There are literally times you feel like you're going to drown in the sorrow.

There was a time when I felt "the PEACE" that surpasses all understanding.

Recently, we learned the governor of California changed some laws, and now the man incarcerated for Lynette's death is eligible for parole. Though I've been given the prompting from the Holy Spirit to "be anxious for nothing," my entire being struggled with this new cyclone of events.

I'd wanted to submit a story for this book but wasn't sure I could. Then, in just a few days, I received encouraging messages, texts, and phone calls from family and friends, all having something to do with PEACE!

A favorite place for me to go and pray, write, and take pictures is called Faith, Hope, and Charity Vineyard. I planned on going there to write a Victim's Impact Statement, hoping the peaceful atmosphere would help.

God miraculously calmed this storm. The inmate waived his hearing for a year.

I heed the words of our dear Savior, "PEACE, Be Still!"

We have peace with God through
our Lord Jesus Christ.

Romans 5:1

Finding Peace in God's Promise

by Rutez Mason

I've walked through storms that could have swallowed me whole. Betrayal, heartbreak, loss, and fear tried to write my ending. But God rewrote the script.

There were days I cried myself to sleep and nights I stayed awake wondering if I'd survive the next blow. I've buried dreams, delivered a stillborn daughter, and faced the possibility of a diagnosis that could have changed everything. I've been lied to, used, and left to pick up the pieces alone. But I was never truly alone.

In the quiet moments, when no one else understood, God whispered, "I got you." And He did.

Peace didn't come because everything was perfect. It came because I stopped trying to control the outcome and started trusting the One who already knew it. I found peace in prayer. Peace in the Word. Peace in the arms of my children. Peace in the strength I didn't know I had.

I learned that peace isn't the absence of pain. It's the presence of God in the middle of it. It's the ability to smile while the winds howl. To laugh while healing. To love again without fear. Now, I walk with a quiet confidence. Not because life is easy, but because I know who holds me. I'm not bitter. I'm better. I'm not broken. I'm built. I'm not afraid because peace lives here in my heart, in my home, and in my story. If God gave it to me, He will give it to you, too.

His Daily Gift of Peace
by Rebecca Ellen Laird

The sun was low in the sky. Outside our window, traffic grew quieter. I used to love the way the light hit our vertical blinds, before the diagnosis. Now, sunset meant night was coming, and with it, the fear. Fear so hard it knocked my knees together. Our appointment was in the morning. My husband, just 23 years old.

It was the waiting that got to us. The lights would go out, and we would try to sleep. But peace, we knew, would not come.

"Do not fear." "Do not let your hearts be troubled..." There it is, hundreds of times. Our Bible-college minds were trying to absorb the fact that Tedd was sick. It was Hodgkin's, Stage Four. Weren't we here in Detroit to launch into ministry? Just four months into marriage, in a strange new city, we found ourselves in the middle of a fight for his life.

It was during these first weeks that we learned what these verses really mean: "...Do not worry about tomorrow ... Sufficient for the day is its own trouble." (Matt. 6:34, NKJV)

In the morning, our alarm would ring, announcing the new day. We were breathing more deeply now. A sense of vigor arose to meet the challenge. The gift of peace had arrived.

The Lord gave us this gift through our horrible experience. We could focus on the troubles ahead or trust that the Lord would meet us with faith for that day.

Once we had mastered this, we no longer lived in fear. Only God could quell my fearful heart.

He can quiet yours, too, with His daily gift of peace.

Making peace through his blood,
shed on the cross.

Colossians 1:20

An Encounter with an Angel of Peace
by Sharlotte Brian

...the peace of God, which surpasses all understanding,
will guard your hearts and your minds in Christ Jesus.
Philippians 4:7, ESV

As a 20-year-old backseat passenger in a car, I suddenly felt my body being gently drawn into a safe, comfortable place. Then, I sensed a profound presence to my left. I turned and saw a Being of Light illuminating the entire left side of the car. This magnificent Being radiated a brilliant white light, focusing all its power on me. It looked at me with all of the love of God and the entire Universe, leaving me breathless and in complete awe.

This incredible Angel, as I later called it, appeared before me in shimmering robes of dazzling white light that glistened from within. The robe formed the figure of a human, radiating pure white light. Its robe shimmered like liquid diamond fabric, and each thread seemed alive. Then, the bell-shaped sleeves opened, stretching out its arms, and it gestured toward me. Then the Angel spoke directly into my mind, saying very, very clearly and slowly that "Everything… is going to be okay." The words unleashed their power within me, and I was enveloped in a profound sense of peace. The peace that I prayed for as a child. Peace like I had never known before. Peace that was tangible and infilling. It felt as if all my cells were called to attention all at once. Each cell became an ember, touched by a spark of Divine energy. This feeling washed through my body like waves, until every cell settled into serene divinity. Then it disappeared as quickly as it had appeared, changing my life forever.

Resource: *Do You See What I See: True Stories of My Prophetic Visions* by Sharlotte J Brian

YOU ARE enough

May Peace Be With Me

by Sally Mary de Leon

There was a time when my life looked fine on the outside but felt like a war zone on the inside. Smiles covered the exhaustion. Laughter drowned the ache. And silence — my silence — carried the weight of every unspoken wound. I had to learn that peace wasn't something to stumble upon; it was something I would have to create, one choice at a time.

Peace began for me the day I got tired of carrying what was breaking me. I stood in front of the mirror and told myself, You cannot heal while holding on to what hurt you. So I began to lay things down — the hurt, the grudges, the disappointments, the voices in my head that told me I wasn't enough or worthy.

Peace as a practice. Each morning became an invitation to choose stillness and calm over chaos. I pictured the life I longed for — a steady mind, a safe home, relationships grounded in love, and a heart free from rehearsing its pain.

I've learned the path isn't always straight. Some days, old habits and hurts return, uninvited. When that happens, I meet myself with grace instead of judgment. Forgiving myself is a superpower. Each time I rise after stumbling, peace grows deeper roots.

Boundaries became my lifeline. "Yes" for what builds me. "No" for what drains me. With every sunrise, I choose to live in peace. I trust peace will stay as long as I keep choosing it—and as long as I keep forgiving myself on the days I stumble.

But the meek shall inherit the earth; and shall delight themselves in the abundance of peace.

Psalm 37:11

Peace Lives Inside
by Rev. Sandra Kitt

My first conscious thought was "What the hell happened?" Waking up with tubes sticking out of every part of my body, unable to move, talk, or swallow. It was difficult to breathe since I had aspiration pneumonia. I remember a visit from my minister, Rev. Temple Hayes, when she asked me if I was ready to get out of there.

I responded, "YES" by winking and moving my knuckle on the little finger. The healing began once I chose LIFE.

Nothing prepares you for this type of challenge. After five months in the hospital doing physical, occupational, and speech therapy daily, I went home. Home is where the mental challenges began. Sleep was incredibly difficult, coming begrudgingly in three to four-hour blocks.

As a chaplain, I knew how helpful meditation could be. First, I needed to be able to concentrate again. It took over a year. I started by reading, doing small puzzles, and playing brain games on the computer.

When I first started meditating, I had trouble focusing on my breath and could only go for a few minutes at a time. I gradually added time and experimented with several different types of meditation.

One thing I know for sure is that when I take the time to go inside, I am so much more grateful and loving. This continues to get me through life's challenges and fosters PEACE within me and the world around me.

God's Unshakable Presence

by Donna Guary

Be strong and courageous. Do not be afraid or terrified
because of them, for the Lord your God goes with you;
He will never leave you nor forsake you.
Deuteronomy 31:6 (NIV)

Have you noticed the saying "Faith over Fear"? It's everywhere: t-shirts, mugs, billboards, etc. Have you thought about what it means? Life has a way of bringing us face-to-face with uncertainty—unexpected changes, challenges, or even fears that keep us awake at night. In those moments, the call from Scripture is clear and unwavering: *Be strong and courageous.*

This is not a suggestion; it's a reminder rooted in the truth that we are never alone. In Deuteronomy 31:6, Moses speaks these words to Israel as they prepare to enter the Promised Land without him. The task before them was daunting, yet the assurance was greater: *The Lord your God goes with you; He will never leave you nor forsake you.*

That same promise stands true for us today. His promise doesn't expire when life gets hard, and our circumstances don't shake His peace. God's promise — *"I will never leave you nor forsake you"* isn't just for Bible times. It's for today, tomorrow, and every day ahead. His presence is our peace, rooted in the certainty that He will never abandon us—it is a gift we can carry into every moment.

Where in your life do you need to lean into God's presence and His peace today instead of leaning into fear?

Prayer: Lord, thank You for always being with me. When fear rises, remind me of Your presence. Give me the strength and courage to walk forward, knowing You will never leave or forsake me. Amen

Peace be with you!

John 20:21

Peace in the Storm

by Tyra Glaze

God never leads us into a storm that
He doesn't give us the power to overcome.
John Bevere

Dear God, thank you for being my PEACE whenever I release my worries into your hands. Through every "storm of life," I've felt your presence, which helped me to overcome with faith and resilience. I'm reminded that there is PEACE even in the storm.

The breast cancer diagnosis came in 2013 like a tornado and tried to destroy my body, BUT GOD was my PEACE in the storm. The death of loved ones back to back seemed like severe thunderstorms causing so much rain (tears) and dark clouds, BUT GOD was my PEACE in the storms. After ending a long-term relationship with someone I loved, I became cold-hearted, my heart felt as if I had been in a blizzard, BUT GOD was my PEACE in the storm. I'm sunshine mixed with a little hurricane!

During my "storms of life," I embrace the moment, even the discomfort. I know that GOD is with me through every storm; He is «The Prince of Peace.»

In the middle of your "life's storms," remember that God offers PEACE. When everything else shakes, His PEACE is calm. He is your refuge, your anchor, and your shelter in the storm. Isaiah 26:3 tells us that "He will keep in perfect PEACE those whose minds are steadfast, because they trust in Him." I'm a witness, storms don't last forever!

Where do you need His peace most now?

What is your current storm? Name it. Give it to God!

BE STILL AND KNOW

PEACE by Piece

by Fran Asaro

I remember it as if it were yesterday. Sitting on my couch, back in my old townhouse, alone and introspecting about my divorce and recreating my life.

Along with the myriad of plans I was making —new social activities, a new career, and a new way of being —a moment of clarity had me realize that what I wanted most was a peaceful life.

I grew up in a New York Italian family, where noise and chaos came with the inheritance, then segued into my marriage, where even good days were loud and busy.

Living a peaceful life was a challenge with that as a backdrop.

Yearning for a quieter existence didn't automatically produce one. I had to learn what my version of peace was and what it wasn't. That's where my journey began as I evaluated situations, experiences, conversations, and even fantasies as to which represented peace and which did not.

As I spent some time sorting what I would ultimately store in my library, I began sewing together the patchwork quilt of peace-for-me, and it began to take form.

Nowadays, while it may not be present every day, peace has become a place I can access within, and I am grateful to have found my formula.

For those who feel the pull of having a peaceful life but lack a frame of reference or access to it, I recommend piecing together your version of it one step at a time and starting to build your library.

The LORD blesses his people with peace.

Psalm 29:11

Choosing Trust: Finding God's Peace Through Grief

by Ted Jordan

The scripture, Philippians 4:4-8, comes to mind when we are seeking to obtain God's peace and joy. It reminds us to keep our hearts and minds focused on what His word says and not on our circumstances.

This passage became even more real to me when my bride of almost 35 years, Crystal Yvette Jordan, took her last breath and passed from this life into eternity to be forever with the Lord on June 10th, 2023. At that point, I had to make a decision: either I was going to continue to trust God, knowing full well that He would never leave me or forsake me, or allow myself to be overcome by excruciating grief as my mind raced around like a little child trying to figure out what to do next.

Anyone who has ever lost a spouse knows that once the marital partnership is dissolved, all of the responsibilities that you once shared now come crashing down on you. It was at times a frightening and daunting task. But I chose to continue to trust my Heavenly Father, and He rewarded me with His peace. When you have His peace, you also have the mind of Christ, which means you have clarity of mind. So you can hear His still small voice.

When those waves of grief came, I would allow myself to go through the process of grieving, but I didn't take that trip alone. God the Father was there with me all the way. He's just that BIG, and He's just that AWESOME. Overwhelming victory is ours when we decide to trust and obey God continuously.

HIS GRACE IS *enough*

=2 COR 12:9

Peace From Within
by Debra Costanzo

The pursuit of peace has always been woven into the fabric of our human experience. For centuries, it has been sung about, prayed for, written into poems, and etched into the collective longing of humankind. Songs like "Give Peace a Chance," "Peaceful, Easy Feeling," and "Let There Be Peace on Earth" remind us that the desire for peace is universal. There are countless others, each one an echo of the human heart's yearning.

We often treat peace as something outside ourselves—something to be chased, pondered, and maybe, if we're fortunate, captured. But true peace is not an external prize. It dwells within the deepest part of us—our soul, our spirit. Its presence, or absence, is directly tied to the lens through which we view the world. Peace is not a reaction to circumstances; it is a condition of the heart. It is not dependent on calm surroundings, favorable news, or the absence of struggle. It is either nurtured within… or it is not.

Inner peace, far from being a shallow phrase, is the soil in which all other healthy emotions grow. It can flourish even when life's path is steep or shadowed. Whether we enjoy abundance or scarcity, health or illness, deep love or seasons of loneliness, peace can accompany us through it all. It is best found in the present moment—planning wisely for tomorrow but living fully in today.

Life's gentle gifts can stir peace—the rhythmic voice of ocean waves, the cry of gulls above the shore, or a quiet rain before dawn. A walk under autumn's golden canopy or a sky blanketed in white clouds may awaken it. Yet peace, even in its quietest form, already lives within a heart that meets each new day with gratitude, grace, and mercy.

And the peace of God, which passeth all understanding, shall keep your hearts and minds through Christ Jesus.

Philippians 4:7

The Power of Peace

by Eileen Bild

Is...
It possible for inner peace?
A way to wake up from
A long, long sleep.

Perhaps...
It will begin, when each
Individual looks within,
For their spark of light
Only they can ignite.

Inner...
Peace is ready for the taking
To rise to the top
Not to be forsaken.

A...
Ripple will be felt
Once the tides have turned.
Those who are close by,
Are the lucky ones.

The...
Power of peace can be felt
For miles around.
Once it has started, fast
Feet have hit the ground.

Running...
Against the tick of the clock,
As the energy of peace
Does not wish to stop.

Take...
A moment, sit back and relax
Measure the level your inner
Peace has become.

FIND INNER PEACE
Happy Mind

Bucket List #10

by Ruth Holly Currey

When I decided to add Disneyland Paris to my list, I didn't realize how important that decision would end up being to me and my healing and grieving process.

As you read in my previous posts, the beginning of this trip had been rough. With the strikes in Paris, we didn't get to experience some of the things we had planned. However, although I didn't post about it, there was another thing that was occurring within my family that was occupying my thoughts. For the past couple of weeks, my mom has been in the hospital. I had visited her right before I left for Paris. I continued to keep her and my dad in my thoughts, but she made me promise that I would go and enjoy every bit of the trip that I had been planning for so long.

Unfortunately, as we arrived at the Disney hotel and got checked in, I received the word that my mother had passed away. I didn't know how to feel. My brain just stopped. After many tears, messages, calls, hugs, and everything we could possibly think of, we decided to go into the parks and wander. I needed air, and I needed to find some comfort in the chaos. Disney has always been a huge part of my life, and I find comfort in being surrounded by the music, the characters, and everything it brings with it. I needed to be surrounded by something that not only brought joy into my life, but was also something I shared with my mom. Disney brought her so much joy, too. I needed to be enveloped by it. So that's what we did. We stayed out late and made the most of our first day together by allowing Disney to let us grieve in a safe and familiar place.

After an incredibly hard and emotional day, we spent the entire day today out and about in the parks. It was warm and the lines were long, but we managed to ride everything we were trying to ride and experience. However, there was one moment that was completely unplanned and ended up making my entire day.

We were in the process of walking from Adventure Land to Tomorrowland. As we passed in front of the castle, I heard Flitterin' begin to play over the speakers. Nowhere else in the entire Disney universe, and never in a million years, did I ever expect to hear a song from the Disney classic Summer Magic play. To most people in the park, this was background noise, and I would be willing to bet that most couldn't name that tune, much less the movie it was from. But, you know who would recognize it? Me...and my mom...

When that song played, I knew for a fact that my mom was there with me. She was so excited to know that I was going on this trip, and as much as I hate being away from my family during this time, my mom got to share that moment in front of the castle with me. That song cannot be at the top of the list of songs that randomly play. That song was played for me, and it was played for my mom.

One of the lines from the song that I love and I find to be incredibly relevant (especially today) is, "New places, new faces, new friendships will start.... While old places, old faces, stay dear to our hearts."

Flitterin' - Summer Magic 1963

There are no words to describe how I am feeling right now, and I cannot accurately explain how much I love my mom and how much I already miss her. But, for anyone who truly knew her, you will understand how important this decision was for me to have this on my list. This wasn't just about me going to another Disney park. This ended up being exactly what I needed to begin to grieve, to begin to heal, and share another new Disney experience with my mom.

> *If there ever comes a day when we can't be together,*
> *keep me in your heart.*
> *I'll stay there forever.*
> **A.A. Milne**

A Prayer for Peace in a World of Distractions
by Kimberly Eddy

I hear You whisper: "Be still, and know that I am God."
God of all comfort, I pray for peace in my anxious heart. Still my racing thoughts and quiet my restless spirit.

Give me wisdom to know when to engage and when to rest. Teach me the sacred rhythm of work and resting in You.

Grant me the courage to choose presence over productivity. Help me value being with You over endless doing.

When my mind races with worry, remind me You hold all things together.

When I'm tempted to scroll away my anxiety, draw me instead to Your word and Your presence.

When I feel overwhelmed by all I haven't done, write on my heart that I am loved, not for my productivity, but simply because I am Yours.

Remind me to choose peace over performance. To choose rest over rushing. To choose Your rhythm over the world's demands.

Work in my heart to practice the discipline of attention, attending to You, to others, to the present moment You have given me.

I will embrace the rhythm of rest, trusting that You sustain the world even when my hands are still .

I remember that my worth is not measured by my productivity or popularity. Continually remind me I am Your beloved child, created for connection, not consumption, called to peace, not performance.

(Bible References: Psalm 46:10, Psalm 94:19, Psalm 127:2, Matthew 11:28-30, Hebrews 4:9-10, Colossians 1:17, Isaiah 26:3, Luke 12:22-26, Romans 5:5, Hebrews 12:2, Philippians 4:8, 2 Corinthians 4:18, Ecclesiastes 3:1-11)

And my people shall dwell in a peaceful habitation, and in sure dwellings, and in quiet resting places.

Isaiah 32:18

Dwelling in His Peace

by Denise C. Herndon Harvey

There is so much taking place in the world today, and often it can be hard to hear the soft voice of the Holy Spirit within, yet it is so very necessary for our peace, and not just for our peace, but for our daily guidance. It does not take much to become so involved, and very frustrated, and perhaps even fearful, as we see with our natural eyes, chaos and danger all around us. However, the Word of God reminds us He has already given us the peace we need to live and accomplish in this world. Discover this peace in your seeking, and in the presence of Holy Spirit, and especially when we become anxious or perhaps doubting, when we are looking more at the world, than in the Word of God.

When we seek out a place where we can sit alone, with our eyes closed, and just envision how it feels to have the Comforter, fill our space with the love from the Father, we will experience the inner knowing, that we are loved, protected, wanted, guided, and exactly where we should be. We can rest in that knowledge of who He is in our life, and the inner peace He has for all of His children.

God's Prescription for Peace
by Jo Ann Walczak

"**D**id you thank Mrs. Davis for the special art lesson, Claire?" Dad asked.

"Yes, I said, 'Thank you.' "

"Good job, Claire, but remember you said it once, but *you can never say thank you enough*. Let's get a card for Mrs. Davis, and you can send her a thank-you note, too."

Truth: We can never say thank you enough, especially when the thanks belongs to God.

Saying "thank you," often and generously, is an attitude game-changer. What demons of the mind can stand against a steady diet of thankfulness?

- Thank you, I have a job, and it pays my bills.
- Thank you for my 2010 Chevy. It still gets me to work.
- Thank you, I have never gone hungry.
- Thank you for a kind friend like Gloria.

Keep the "thank-yous" going, moment-by-moment, day-after-day.

- Thank you, Lord, that You are always with me.
- Thank you for forgiving me.

Thankfulness leads directly to peace. A grateful attitude transforms negativity and adjusts our perspective. The focus shifts from "Woe is me!" to "Whoa! I'm blessed!" Thankfulness must be intentional, a continual watchfulness for the joys we often overlook in our adversity. Exchanging complaints and grievances for gratitude and contentedness in our situations is the catalyst for peace.

Thankfulness is God's prescription for peace: "… in every situation, by prayer and petition, WITH THANKSGIVING, present your requests to God. And the peace of God, which transcends all understanding, will guard your hearts and minds in Christ Jesus." Philippians 4:6-7 (NIV)

Thank you, Lord, for giving me peace.

Choose Peace

By Mary Vovers Brown

The sun rose gently, casting a soft golden glow across the kitchen table. She cradled her mug, watching steam curl into the morning light. Today was quiet. Still. No chaos, no demands—just breath and the quiet hum of life outside.

She had spent so long fighting. Fighting to hold on, fighting to be enough. But lately, something inside her whispered: What if you didn't have to fight at all?

Her phone buzzed. A message from someone she'd let go. A door she had once begged to keep open. She stared at it, not with sadness, but with a sense of peace. That chapter had taught her much. But it was over. And that was okay.

In the stillness, she felt it: a deep knowing that growth sometimes means releasing, not clinging. That some doors must close for better ones to appear. That her journey—imperfect, winding, hers alone—was unfolding exactly as it should.

She looked out the window, watching leaves drift down, letting go with such grace. Nature didn't resist change. Why should she?

She took another breath. No grand declarations. No dramatic turning points. Just a quiet decision made over a warm cup and soft morning light: I choose peace. Not just today. Every day.

Peace in letting go.
Peace in starting again.
Peace in the in-between.

Maybe, just maybe, she was exactly where she needed to be—learning, growing, becoming.

And he shall speak peace unto the heathen: and his dominion shall be from sea even to sea, and from the river unto the ends of the earth.
Zecharia 9:10

The Sacred Practice Of Peace
by Michelle Harwood-Lange

B ack in January 2021, I wrote: "Life is changing rapidly. If I don't adapt, I risk being consumed by negativity." That truth still echoes. Peace begins by naming the patterns that disrupt it—and choosing differently.

I've learned to listen to my inner compass, to stop editing my truth to fit the realm of "should be." Peace is a practice. A devotion. A way of being.

As a parent of a neurodivergent child, I've felt the drain of BIG EMOTIONS.

On a day of "pancake stacking," I became dysregulated. With support, I learned it's okay to pause, to breathe, to honor my nervous system as sacred ground. By seeing my daughter's divine light—and honoring my own—I shape my choices with grace.

In my sanctuary, I keep a journal, scripture, and books of wisdom. There, I listen, reflect, and remember who I am. *Be still and know that I AM* is my conduit.

In stillness, I expand my mustard seed faith and connect with God's power to restore peace.

Peace is a seed I choose to grow. My mission is clear: do not allow anything—including myself—to disturb it. I've learned: **Anger never persuades. Control does not influence.**

- So, I create space to live for my future now.
- Take a break.
- Breathe.
- Find the good in you.
- Capture your quiet power.
- Let faith remind you: **You are whole**.

I'VE GOT

This

LUKE 1:37

Peace After the Unthinkable
by Glenis McEwen Moss

When my husband's sudden death shattered my life, God's promises became my anchor and His peace my lifeline.

On Sunday, July 28, 2019, my husband, Ralph, and I were getting ready for church. I was making tea and gathering my guitar; he was getting his music for the piano. Suddenly, he called me over. "I have a strange pain in my back," he said. Minutes later, as I spoke with the 911 operator, Ralph reached for my hand and prayed aloud:

Dear Heavenly Father, if there is any unconfessed sin in my life, forgive me, wash me clean, and please take care of my sweet wife. Give her strength.

Those were the last words I heard him pray. By 11:15 AM, Ralph had gone home to meet his Savior.

That night, I lay in bed, my heart shattered. "Lord, I don't understand," I prayed. "I'm a widow at 62 with no children. Our dreams for the future are gone. But I want to honor You and Ralph. Give me strength for this next chapter."

The next morning, I opened my Bible, and my eyes fell on Isaiah 57:1–2 (NLT): *The godly often die before their time... God is protecting them from the evil to come... those who follow godly paths will rest in peace when they die.*

Through tears, I made a choice: to believe that promise. I began writing down reasons to be grateful Ralph was with the Lord, and I clung to His Word—Jeremiah 29:11, Deuteronomy 31:8, Philippians 4:13.

That decision brought peace. Over the next three years, God turned my pain into purpose—through songwriting, creating a widows' coaching program, and later, marrying a wonderful godly man named Gary.

I've learned this: When we surrender our deepest sorrow to God, He redeems it. His peace doesn't erase the loss—but it carries you through, one step at a time.

*For unto us a child is born, unto us a son
is given: and the government shall be upon
his shoulder: and his name shall be called
Wonderful, Counsellor, The mighty God, The
everlasting Father, The Prince of Peace.*

Isaiah 9:6

Can I Get An Amen
by Will Pollock

RuPaul signs off every *Drag Race* episode with "If you can't love yourself, how the hell are you gonna love somebody else... Can I get an amen?"

Ru's true-ism also applies to peace: If we don't consciously create inner peace for ourselves (a place of refuge for tough times), our ability to coexist in a world fraught with turmoil will be far more difficult.

If life stressors were landmines, inner peace gives us the agility to avoid explosions and continue on our journey.

The question
Some months ago, my 6-year-old son Cam looked up in the kitchen and pointed. "Daddy, why is there a TV on the wall, and why is it never on?" To which I replied, "Well, about 10 years ago I used to have news on while cooking... but not anymore."

In that moment, I realized that inactive TV fostered serenity and bolstered my inner peace. Instead of cable news spoiling the center of our life, I was able to be fully present, teaching my son how to make bagels from scratch. I was distraction-free filming one of his hilarious moments, sucking a lemon or trying vinegar for the first time—without corporate news yipping in the background.

As a trained journalist, I've become jaded by ratings and profit-polluting news. I grew up watching Peter Jennings, the gold standard of anchors, before everything went to hell. The proliferation of 24-hour news has—and I will die on this hill—made Americans dumber and definitely *not* more informed.

Kitchen memories

So yep, that TV gathering dust on the wall is an old relic from past routines. And it will stay off. After all, if we measure "emotional souvenirs" a family creates in certain rooms of the home, the kitchen will be at the top of everyone's list.

Author and cancer survivor Kris Karr once said, "When you're the conscious captain in your kitchen, you'll feel better mentally and physically." That's true, and if we want to keep making new memories, it's best to keep TVs off.

Can I get an amen?

Prayer for Healthy Boundaries for Strong, Peace-filled Relationships
Author Unknown

Dear God, please give me guidance and wisdom to
establish healthy boundaries in my relationships.
I recognize the importance of setting boundaries that
honor both myself and the other person.

Father, help me to have the courage to communicate
my needs and desires, while also respecting the
boundaries of others.
Teach me to discern when boundaries have been crossed
and give me the strength to address these
situations with love and grace.
Please grant me the wisdom to know when to say no,
when to say yes, and when to seek Your guidance.
May my relationships be built on mutual respect,
trust, and understanding.

I surrender my relationships to You,
trusting that You will guide me in establishing
healthy boundaries that bring glory to Your name.
Amen.

The Ingredients of Peace
by Sally Mary de Leon

I can see my grandmother, even in the midst of life's storms, carrying a calm presence like a warm blanket. She once told me, "Peace is not found — it's grown inside you, watered by what you choose to see and believe."

Peace is the quiet pulse of a life in harmony with itself, the steady heartbeat of someone at rest in their spirit. It is breathing deeply with confidence in what is to come and exhaling with gratitude for the path already traveled.

Peacefulness lives in the feeling of safety, in dwelling fully in the present moment with trust in the future and reverence for the lessons of the past. The mind and heart move together as one, each step aligned, each breath a choice toward calm.

Peace thrives where trust is rooted. Trust in God (or Your higher power), knowing a greater presence guides each step. Trust in yourself, embracing the strength and wisdom to navigate every challenge. Trust in your community, where your presence is cherished and your absence leaves a meaningful space.

Gratitude enriches peace. It sees the blessings in a warm meal, the unexpected joy of a friend's call, and the golden promise of the sunrise. Gratitude collects these moments as treasures, creating a foundation strong enough to carry you through seasons of change into seasons of abundance.

Peace is chosen daily. The tides of life rise and fall, yet you decide how to stand — anchored, grounded, and resilient, certain that calm always follows the storm.

I will hear what God the LORD will speak: for he will speak peace unto his people, and to his saints; but let them not turn again to folly.

Psalm 85:8-9

Peace is as Peace Does
by Candi Parker

Let's be honest—most of us have had those moments where we look at our life and think, *something's gotta change*. But here's the twist: life doesn't change while we're twiddling our thumbs waiting. It changes when we do—quietly, intentionally, and often in the tiniest of steps.

The truth is, every day hands us a buffet of reasons to think negatively. One rude comment, one bad headline, one burnt piece of toast—and suddenly we're swept into the storm. So, how do you turn this ship around? How do you build a life that feels more peaceful, more grounded, more *yours*?

You start by feeding yourself peace—daily, like breakfast for your soul. Mornings are your secret weapon. Before the world barges in with its noise, claim a few minutes for stillness. Read something uplifting. Watch a short, inspiring video. Open your window and let the birds sing to you.

Peace builds like muscle—you strengthen it through repetition. This is about re-training your brain to choose calm over chaos, to see possibilities instead of problems.

Think of your thoughts like an energetic puppy. At first, they dart around, pulling you toward every distraction. But with gentle, steady training, they learn to stay, to settle, and to follow your lead. The more you practice, the easier it gets to live from a peaceful center—even on messy days.

Here's the real secret: You transform your life by showing up for yourself every day—choosing peace again and again until it becomes second nature. Because peace isn't just something you "find." It's something you practice. It's something you *become*.

So be kind to others. Be kind to yourself. Be peace.

Be the
LIGHT

MATTHEW 5:14

Peace Begins in the Grocery Store

by Karen Mayfield

While standing in the checkout line at the store one day, I was part of a universal exercise in giving for giving, paying it forward, and passing it on.

When the cashier handed the lady in front of me her change, $3.45, a little boy, who was about seven, appeared and asked the lady if she could spare her change. The coin total was 45 cents. He told her he was hungry and his mom, his two brothers, and his sister needed help. The lady was so mean to the little boy, promptly telling him it was wrong to beg. The cashier apologized for the child, stating that he was in the store every day asking for money, but usually, he's not that bold.

At that point, I couldn't stand what I was hearing, so I chimed in with, "I was thinking that this little boy is going to be a great businessman one day because of this training he is getting as a child." I didn't see him as bold; I saw him as brave, but more importantly, I recognized that the child was allowing me to give for giving, no conditions, no expectations, and certainly no judgment.

I was amazed at what followed… I gave, and the lady in front of me gave her change, plus several more dollars. The person behind me gave. A "Pro-action" of giving for giving, paying it forward, and passing it on began. When the ripple of giving stopped, the little boy had plenty of money to buy groceries, and someone even helped him get the groceries home.

Tears of JOY streamed down my face...this is what being human is all about. So the next time the Universe presents the opportunity to give, pay close attention. Don't miss it; you could start a chain of "Pro-action." The more we help others, the greater the ripple effect of collaboration, and the sooner we bring PEACE.

*And let the peace of God rule in your hearts,
to the which also ye are called in one body;
and be ye thankful.*

Colossians 3:15

I Am Not Angry

by Angi Currier

Eight months ago, I lost my son to suicide. He was 33 years old. He had a two-year-old daughter and a fiancé. He had been dealing with depression for a long time. He would take his medications for it, and then when he felt better, he would stop. I reconnected with him after twenty years of not being able to have any contact with him because he and my daughter were kept from me.

After we reconnected and got to know each other, he knew I never stopped loving him or trying to reach out. He was very angry when he found out. He didn't know how to control his anger. He wanted just to be loved. He had the biggest heart and was fun to be around. Every time we saw each other and hugged, it was like he was a little boy again. He would just sob on my shoulder. He was hurting, and I didn't know how to fix it or make things better for him.

He formed a bond with his little sister, who knew about him, but he didn't know about her. They loved being together. We all knew he was struggling with depression, and he didn't want to be a burden to anyone. He felt like he was always an outcast growing up. We included him in everything after reconnecting. We were his family. The morning I got the call that he had taken his life the night before, as much as it hurt me and the ones who loved him, I understood. I wasn't angry with him. I wasn't questioning the why. I knew. I knew deep in my soul that he was finally at peace, and in that moment, so was I.

Uncovering Peace
by Rachelle Simpson Sweet

The world roars, screens flashing, voices calling, clocks ticking. Life rushes past in a blur, and I forget to notice my own breath.

Then I step away from this world. Under the giant oak, the air shifts. The wind carries the scent of wildflowers, the sun spills gold across my skin, and the rustle of leaves becomes a lullaby. The noise loosens its grip, melting like mist in the first light of day.

In the gap between thoughts, there is only presence, this moment in time, nothing else. The earth hums beneath me, steady and unshaken, and I remember that I belong to something greater than the rush.

For me, being in nature is my medicine. I notice the way sunlight scatters across the forest floor, painting shifting patterns in gold and shadow. I imagine fairies or spirits dancing whimsically. My thoughts, so restless in the working world, rushing from one task to the next, making lists, checking boxes, feeling the pressure of worldly demands begin to diminish in importance.

Sometimes I find myself by a stream, the water tumbling over smooth stones, its rhythm unhurried and certain. It mirrors the passage of all nature: the rush, the fall, the still, and the stagnant. Nature doesn't care about my schedules or worries; it moves to its own timeless pulse. And somehow, in its presence, those pressures melt away, returning my sanity and, at times, a surprising clarity of thought. It is as if the scattered puzzle pieces of my mind fall into place.

Peace, I've learned, isn't something we chase; it's something we uncover when we step into the space between our thoughts. Nature holds the doorway to its discovery, and breath brings it into us. And inside, there is only presence, vast, still, timeless.

Peace I leave with you,
my peace I give unto you:
not as the world giveth, give I unto you.

John 14:27

Breaking the Cycle to Live in Peace
by Andrea Giammolvo

A verbally abusive parent can steal a child's peace at any time, simply by demeaning them. Now, at 68 years of age, I no longer feel the fear that for so much of my younger life took the place of peace in my small world.

To balance things out, I became a "people pleaser". I did whatever it took: Being funny and saying yes to things I wished I hadn't, to feel accepted, and in a sense, loved.

God, in his miraculous way, brought my polar opposite husband into my life when I was 21. His presence was always reassuring and non-judgmental, which didn't erase who I had already become, but slowly helped me become whole.

Upon word of my pregnancy for each of my children, I, of course, prayed for a healthy baby, but moreover for my children to have "peace of mind". To me, that would give them the most valuable gift in life, one that I never had, and was still in the process of finding. But to be honest, I needed faith, guidance, and hard work to overcome some of the genetic personality traits I inherited.

My two adult children are now raising self-assured, respectful children of their own, who wake up happy and are ready for the world. They accept the challenges of life, knowing the soft and fuzzy reassurance is always there waiting for them. THIS gives me peace. The cycle is broken, and it is evident that God answered my prayers.

What a gift…..

BE STRONG
BE BRAVE
BE FEARLESS
JOSHUA 1:9

Manifesting Peace

by Barbara Yager

If you ask people what they want for the world, they often respond with, "World Peace". Yes, that would be a wonderful state of being.

But, to bring World Peace into being, it requires that we find our own personal state of Peace. We can't manifest what we don't feel.

Personal peace can be an elusive state for many of us. We live in a world that has many challenges that diminish a peaceful state of being. How can we find that peaceful state of mind? It's easy, create a focus for it in your life.

The first thing you need to do is to take a personal stock of the level of peace in your life. On a scale of 1 to 10, where do you land, with 10 being the most peaceful? I am guessing you might land around 3 or 4 on the peace scale.

Peace in our hearts is a vibrational state we can manifest. We manifest everything in our lives. From the lunch we ate today to the vacation we wish to take. To manifest peace, we need to focus on creating situations in our lives that can bring us closer to that blissful state of being, called peace.

The quickest way to manifest peace is to become 10 years old again, when we had no responsibilities other than to be a kid. Go back to a time where we were not changed by the collective consciousness and forced to forget about the importance of embodying the power and perfection of personal peace.

Spend part of everyday remembering the Peace in your life, when you were 10. If we all practice remembering, World Peace might not be far off.

Therefore being justified by faith, we have peace with God through our Lord Jesus Christ.

Romans 5:1

Surrender is Where our Path to Serenity Begins

by Michael Starr

The current state of our culture, with the amount of conflict and hatred, is tragic. Empathy and compassion have faded as core cultural values and are increasingly replaced with intolerant and self-righteous divisiveness. Civil debate is being replaced by shouting over one another and efforts to censor opposing views. The idea of agreeing to disagree is rapidly being lost.

Many today suffer profoundly. This suffering manifests itself in anger, despondency, conflict, anxiety, hatred, and crime. However, this suffering can be markedly mitigated when we see and embrace reality for what it is. There is a way to live life as a dance, with a slow crescendo of empowering music in our head that fills our thoughts and convictions with hope and excitement. The paths we take toward this heaven on Earth begin with our ability and willingness to not only accept, but to embrace and surrender to the "What Is" of reality.

Seeing that we cannot control others but rather that we have a degree of influence over them can shift our focus to building and maintain healthy relationships. When we surrender to reality, we stop fighting a futile battle with the fact that things will not always be as we wish them to be. By stopping this fight with "What Is" we free ourselves from a prison battle field that releases us from the shackles of ego & self-righteousness.

Let go of your death grip with how you want things to be and embrace the reality of how things are … work with that. Resistance to reality is futile. Surrender will stop the suffering and allow you to begin your journey toward peace, progress and healing.

RISE
UP & PRAY
LUKE 22:46

Daily Gift of Peace
by January Liddell

A sigh of relief washes over me whenever I think of God. Knowing He is by my side is the light that carries me through each day and the reminder that I am never alone.

When I wake, I long to see His Word reminding me, "I can do all things through Christ who strengthens me" (Philippians 4:13). With mushroom coffee in hand, I scroll through my Bible App's Daily Refresh. In these quiet moments, I open my heart, leaning in to hear His still small voice whisper what I need for the day ahead.

As I read, His peace washes over me—not the fragile peace the world offers, but the steady, unshakable calm that comes only from Him. It is the peace of Philippians 4:7, "which surpasses all understanding." I can't explain it, but I've felt it steady me in life's fiercest storms, the ones that could have swallowed me whole.

I've faced days when fear lied and defeat seemed certain. Yet every time I sought Him first, His peace wrapped me like an invisible hug, gently assuring me, "Everything will be ok."

This daily gift is neither flashy nor loud. It doesn't erase my trials, but it gives me courage, confidence, and grace to walk through them, knowing my God is bigger than any problem I face.

So, each morning when I rise and each night as I lay my head down, my first and last thoughts are of Him—my beginning and my end, my anchor in chaos, my forever friend. Through Him I find peace, and through Him I know I am loved, seen, and safe.

*For I know the thoughts that
I think toward you,
saith the LORD, thoughts of peace,
and not of evil, to give you an expected end.*

Jeremiah 29:11

Peace Through Truth
by Mariena Johnson

S ome say ignorance is bliss—a phrase that traces back to Thomas Gray's 1742 poem, where he wrote, "Where ignorance is bliss, 'tis folly to be wise." For centuries, that line has carried weight, suggesting that sometimes it is easier, even preferable, not to know the truth.

Maybe for some, that sentiment rings true. But for me, I have always been a truth seeker. For me, truth is bliss—however good or bad that truth may be. I subscribe to the belief that the truth will set you free, and in freedom, at least for me, there is peace.

I also believe that wisdom is bliss—and that it can never be "folly to be wise".

Some say ignorance is bliss. I learned that phrase came from Thomas Gray's poem, written back in 1742, with the line: *"Where ignorance is bliss, 'tis folly to be wise."* It's a sentiment that has survived centuries, as if the world wants to remind us that knowledge often comes with burdens.

Maybe for some, that sentiment rings true, but I have never seen it that way. For as long as I can remember, I have been drawn towards truth, even when it stung. To me, truth has always been bliss. Freedom lies in knowing what is real—not in pretending otherwise.

Wisdom, too, has always been my compass. Wisdom feels like a lantern in the dark, illuminating my choices, protecting me from illusions. My path is to know, to seek, to understand. And though it is heavier at times, it is richer too. For me, truth and wisdom are not burdens—they are blessings.

From Fear to Freedom
by Candy Radford

During my twenty-four-year marriage, especially in the last decade, my five children and I endured daily verbal and emotional abuse—yelling, accusations, name-calling, and constant suspicion. Every move I made was monitored and controlled. I had no autonomy as a wife, mother, or even a human being. We walked on eggshells, never knowing when the next explosion would come or what might trigger it. We were always tense—emotionally and physically—never able to relax. The very things that brought us joy were often the ones that enraged him, so we eliminated them from our lives.

Five years ago, we escaped—literally—one day while he was at work. Since then, my children and I have been intent on creating and protecting our peace. Everything we were once forbidden to do—places we couldn't go, people we weren't allowed to see—went on our "Bucket List." At first, we tackled many of these things together as we regained our bearings. Over time, as independence grew, we each spread our wings, discovering peace in our own unique ways.

Knowing we escaped and that my children now have the opportunity to accomplish anything they hope for fills me with joy. We are still healing from the trauma, but we have come so far. My peace is found in reclaiming the things I love—reading, gardening, exercising, teaching—without fear of guilt or repercussions. I have restored cherished friendships, many now my chosen family. Quiet walks in God's creation and soul-refreshing hours on the beach remind me of His steady presence.

I am slowly becoming who I was always meant to be. I am no longer afraid—and that is my greatest peace.

Peacemakers who sow in peace reap
a harvest of righteousness.

James 3:18

Finding Peace in the Everyday

by Martariesa Logue

For a long time, I thought being "busy" was enough. I filled my days with work, volunteering, and endless tasks, thinking that effort equaled love and care. But in reality, I was giving only fragments of myself—my attention, my energy, my presence—to the people and moments that mattered most. I didn't always notice the quiet ways my busyness hurt those around me.

If I have hurt you and haven't apologized, I pray you can let me know, so you may receive the peace shared throughout the stories in this book. I take responsibility for my part, and I hope this acknowledgment offers a small step toward healing.

I have begun to find true peace. It hasn't erased the challenges, regrets, or distractions that used to weigh on me, but it has changed how I experience them. In the stillness, I can breathe. I can focus on my daughter, on my own healing, and on my relationship with God. Peace comes when I surrender what I cannot control and trust Him fully with the ordinary and unseen moments of my life.

As Romans 15:13 (NIV) reminds us: "May the God of hope fill you with all joy and peace as you trust in him, so that you may overflow with hope by the power of the Holy Spirit." Peace isn't earned through doing more; it's received through presence, surrender, and trust. Even small acts—a pause to listen, a quiet moment of reflection, a humble apology—ripple outward, touching lives in ways we may never fully see.

Peace comes when we let go, trust God fully, and give our hearts, not leftovers, to what truly matters.

Ceremony of Peace

by Amy Olmedo

D ebilitating pain. Incessant swelling. Inexplicable stiffness. Pending diagnosis of cancer. My physical condition was whittling away at my emotional capacity as well as my spirit. I was determined to push through the agony to accomplish my dream, my purpose in life. But how in the hell do I create a retreat for healing when I couldn't even heal myself?

Months passed, and doctors simply pushed poisonous medications and proclaimed, *"You're just getting old, get used to it."* However, there was no official diagnosis. Modern as well as traditional medicine were masking my condition, not finding the origin, or curing it. I made an agreement with myself to take the minimal amount of medication for one year and find a solution.

While drafting a chapter on epigenetics, I surmised my suffering paralleled much suffering in my family. The origin of our pain lay in a sepia colored photograph of an adorable little four-year-old boy wearing braces from his polio. His smile masked the pain of not being able to run free, like all the other boys, as he grew up in a hospital.

I prepared myself for meditation and focused on, *"I love you, and our purpose is one."* Through a mystical journey, I removed the harsh metal braces from his fragile legs and watched him joyfully run through golden fields of wheat. Hot tears poured down my cheeks as I removed the pain from my body, and a jolt of light passed across my chest. Within hours, my pain vanished forever.

Together, we found peace in the power of love and set our spirits free.

The peace of God, which transcends
all understanding.

Philippians 4:7

My Peace

by Katharine Banman

O ur emotions are like a river that flows. This river can flow to prove or flow by peace. God made this river. He designed it to pour His essence into its flow. Peace!

The secret to the flow of peace is the Prince of Peace. Jesus. He poured Himself out upon everything that held a voice to prove itself – the drive to find purpose for self. In its place, He released the purpose for which each person was created – to belong and be loved.

The Prince of Peace reveals to us Father God's love and restores to us what we couldn't achieve. He positions us with peace, by sonship, to pure purpose. As vocation is received and we rise with purpose from glory to glory, there is sanctifying in the wholeness of the journey, from salvation to the fulfilment of purpose. It is the righteousness of Christ Jesus that keeps us sanctified from beginning to end.

Even the falls along the way of learning vocation become a testimony of our Prince of Peace. He, who keeps the position for our river to get back to the flow of His. It is in Him that our purpose abides and resides to finish well.

Peace carries frequency. Our DNA cries for it. It calls us to walk in the purpose of Father God. To live what is on His heart for each one. It desires life with Him. Life that lives glorified forever.

John 14:27, John 16:33, Philippians 4:6-7, 2 Thess.3:16

Zealous Zion Zeal - The garden mount, flows a river, with trees beside it, drinking. The trees have healing in their leaves and fruit for nourishment.

Receive and eat. The zeal of the LORD performs this.

Worship Jesus, The Garden King!

be still

AND KNOW THAT I AM

GOD

PSALM 46:10

Mother's Day Finding Purpose in Peace

by Jessie Tieva

I ronically, I'm writing this post on my birthday, and maybe it's because I am now officially "old" that I feel comfortable sharing more about finding peace.

I realize now that I fought for peace for a long time. It wasn't that I didn't want peace in my life, but instead, I felt that I needed people to like me, understand me, and hear me, and my definition of what I thought "peace" was looks much different than it is.

Like me, in earlier years, most people think peace is agreeing with everyone and everyone around you agreeing and living in harmony. Most people overwhelmingly accept this definition of peace. Some struggles and disagreements go on for years within friendships and families as we try our hardest to "make" the other party understand our point of view. In addition to creating division, it does something more profound to your soul and your time, and these negative engagements will derail your purpose while you are fighting battles and trying to please others and find acceptance.

When I found out about Abel's diagnosis of Trisomy 18, I tried relentlessly to get my family to visit him in the NICU. I wanted them to meet him and to understand how incredible and special he was. Unfortunately, none of my persuasions worked, and he passed away without meeting his grandparents, who lived only 20 minutes from the hospital. Abel's passing left me unbelievably heartbroken with grief, and the loss and rejection I felt from my family overwhelmed me.

Something happened when I finally realized that the only path forward was to release my family and the friends who had all scattered through our NICU experience. I found purpose. My head wasn't clouded anymore with the hope that "someday" I could make them all understand. I had to move on, alone with my husband and children. This was real peace. The clarity came, and so did purpose.

Abel's books were published, and his foundation became official only a few months after he passed away. I never expected his story to make such a dramatic impact and grow at the rate it has. With growth, there have also been numerous negative people, jealous people, people spreading rumors and lies, and others who simply want to take from his mission for their own gain. There have been many times when I considered shutting down the foundation because of these people, but just as I had to do with my family when I kept moving forward without looking for peace in the wrong places, my purpose became clearer. True peace is moving beyond the people.

I run Born Abel along with roughly 35 amazing volunteers. None of us takes a salary or benefit in any way financially. I also homeschool three of my children. I have a rambunctious two-year-old (Abel's twin brother, Oren) and am pregnant with twins. Many people may think I have a team on social media, but it's just me posting a reel while I'm pushing my kids on the swing at the park or making a graphic after I put them to bed.

Additionally, I send our illustrators all the individual pictures of children, organize them by name and diagnosis, select the pictures to be illustrated, write the books, and format each page before it is published. It is a full-time job but without a paycheck. When I encounter negative people, it is sometimes quite difficult to convince myself that it is worth my effort, but I am reminded that my purpose with Born Abel is much larger than a few hurtful people. I am reminded of the REAL definition of peace. It's not agreeing with everyone. It's not convincing the other to support your opinion. It's not winning them over to your side. It's moving on from them.

I have had to move on from many people in my life. It can be challenging in some situations, but when you do, you will see YOUR purpose so much more clearly.

This Mother's Day, let go of the fake version of "peace" and release the desire to have others agree with you. Your purpose is more significant and much more important than those people.

IN THE *waiting*

GOD IS WORKING

Peace Through Strength

by Alyssa Ruge

Born in the United States six months after Ronald Reagan took office, I grew up in the shadow of the Cold War. My grandparents would always tell me that freedom was never free and that weakness invited danger. Later, when I heard President Ronald Reagan speak about "peace through strength," the words struck me. Strength, he said, was not about aggression but about ensuring that no one dared to challenge the freedom and peace we valued.

I carried that philosophy into my own life. When I became an attorney, I noticed how the best way to achieve success was through presenting your case strongly throughout. A strong case gave the most negotiating power. Your opponent always has to know in the back of their mind that if they push, you will definitely shove.

The same principle applies beyond law offices and borders. President Reagan believed that America's moral courage and military readiness discouraged those who sought conflict. I saw that lesson mirrored in my own small world: when I showed strength—calm, steady, and consistent—others felt safe. They knew I would protect fairness, and in that assurance, peace blossomed.

When I think of peace, I do not picture silence or passivity. I picture the kind of peace that comes when strength steadies the ground beneath us, when freedom is guarded by vigilance. When I think of peace, I think of a leader like President Ronald Reagan. I learned in my life that true peace is not the absence of struggle, but the presence of strength that makes aggression unthinkable.

"The Lord gives strength to his people; the Lord blesses his people with peace."

Psalms 29:11

The Glass of Water - A Folklore Lesson
Original Author Unknown

During one lecture, a professor suddenly picked up a glass of water and held it up. He stood there quietly, just holding it, as the students began to glance at each other, waiting for an explanation. Ten minutes passed, and he still didn't lower his arm.

Finally, he asked: "Tell me, how much do you think this glass weighs?"

The students started guessing: "Maybe a couple of ounces!" "Four ounces!" "Five!"

The professor smiled. "Honestly, I don't know either. To find out, we'd have to weigh it. But that's not the real question. What happens if I hold this glass for a few minutes?"

"Nothing," the students replied.

"Right. Now, what if I hold it for an hour?"

"Your arm will start to hurt," one answered.

"Correct. And what if I hold it for a whole day?"

"Your arm will go numb, you'll have severe muscle stress, and paralysis," another student ventured, "and you may even need to go to the hospital!"

"Exactly. But did the weight of the glass change during this time?"

"No," the students answered in unison.

"Then what caused the arm ache and muscle stress?"

The students thought for a moment. "Holding onto the glass," one finally answered.

"Precisely," the professor said, "Life's problems are like this glass of water. Hold them for a while, and nothing happens. Hold them longer, and they begin to hurt. Hold them all day long, and you'll feel paralyzed – incapable of doing anything."

The professor paused, letting the lesson sink in. "It's important to remember to put the glass down."

This story sparked a profound message and a question in my soul. Every aspect of who we are, body, mind, soul, and spirit, is affected by the 'weight' of carrying something that we can easily 'put down' or let go of.

So the question is, what does the glass represent for you? What are you carrying around with you that may be disrupting your peace?

The last line of this folklore, "It's important to remember to put the glass down," reminds me that I have a choice. Do I want to continue to stress over something that I can let go of? Or, can I let go and let God handle it?

Sometimes, it's pressure, whether from within or outside of ourselves, that keeps us thinking that we have to do something about whatever it is that has us in a state of stress and is disrupting our peace.

What would happen if we just let go of what doesn't necessarily belong to us, even when we are holding on to it as though it does?

Put the glass down.

Blessings,
Teresa

A Prayer for Peace in Times of Uncertainty

Author Unknown

Gracious Lord, in times of uncertainty and fear,
I seek your peace that transcends circumstances.
Help me trust in your plan and find
security in your promises.
Quiet my anxious thoughts and fill my heart
with your peace that guards my mind and soul.
I surrender my worries to you,
knowing that you are in control.
In Jesus' name, I pray.
Amen.

The LORD will give strength unto his people;
the LORD will bless his people with peace.

Psalm 29:11

Forgiveness Through Peace
Dr. Teresa Lynch

After a painful falling out with my youngest sister over a special family event, we found ourselves estranged. Each of us was certain we were "right," and because the other could not see it, connection felt impossible. The only solution seemed to be silence. I lived in the Northeast, she in the Southeast, and distance spared us from facing one another.

Yet in the quiet, an uncomfortable weight lived inside me—darkness that felt uncomfortably close to hate. This was not who I was, nor who I wanted to be. I turned to Jesus Christ and prayed for help. I leaned on His promise: *"Peace I leave with you, my friend, my peace I give unto you. Not as the world gives do I give to you; let not your heart be troubled, nor let it be afraid."* I repeated this daily, sometimes many times, whenever anger surfaced.

By spring, reciting that scripture had become so much a part of me that I forgot why I was saying it. Peace had quietly settled in.

Months later, at a family camping trip in Vermont, I sat by the water. My sister approached, hesitant. "I thought we were mad at each other?" she asked. I looked at her, puzzled, unable to summon the memory of offense. "What were we angry about?" I asked. Relief washed over her. We hugged, and the week overflowed with joy.

In reflection, I realized something profound: God had not only answered my prayer, but He had erased the sting of unforgiveness. What I could not force with words or will, His peace accomplished. True peace does not come from striving, but as a gift of grace.

Surrounding You With Love
by Ilene Gottlieb

Have you experienced childhood trauma? Are you seeking inner peace? You're not alone!

I was shocked but not surprised that the CDC reported about 64% of adults have experienced childhood trauma involving emotional, physical, or sexual abuse, neglect, or household dysfunction. I was surprised that in the United States, only about 50% of people with PTSD (Post Traumatic Stress Disorder) seek help, and only 58% receive help from a mental health professional. So many people are suffering from trauma and looking for tools for healing.

Hermes Trismegistus said, "As above, so below, as within so without". This suggests that all dysfunction and suffering in the world is being reflected from within each of us. And since we're all connected energetically, we're both affected by this, and the source for the healing.

In all the years I've been a Holistic Nurse and in private practice, I've attracted clients who've experienced everything from mild to horrific traumas. In the beginning, I didn't understand why these were "my people" whom I was here to serve. Then I realized I was attracting them because I was one of them. Anyone who has experienced childhood trauma can't help but have their lives affected. For some, they may have physical symptoms, for others, they may have emotional challenges or relationship issues. For me, whenever anyone touched my back and I didn't "see them coming," it felt like I was jumping three feet off the ground. I didn't realize that was an expression of my PTSD until much later in life.

I searched for years for tools to heal my PTSD from childhood trauma, but it wasn't until I found Ho'oponopono that I was finally able to heal not only myself but also my relationship with my Mom, the source of my trauma. After 67 years of a tumultuous relationship with my Mom and after consistently working with Ho'oponopono for four months, I was blessed with a year and a half of a loving relationship with my Mom before she peacefully transitioned to Spirit.

Ho'oponopono, the ancient Hawaiian problem-solving process, best known by the four phrases "I love you. I'm sorry. Please forgive me. Thank you", was my path to healing and peace, and can be for you as well. Simple yet powerful, by thinking, writing, or speaking the four phrases or just "I love you" or "Thank you" repeatedly, you're asking Divinity to transmute from within you the root cause of your trauma. As Divinity helps you heal your trauma, Divinity continues to transmute the source of your trauma from not only you but from all of Humanity back to the beginning of Creation. That's powerful!

If I was able to heal, so can you. Just start where you are and before you know it, life will be easier, you'll feel more peaceful, and your relationship with yourself and others will change for the better. Choose to begin, and inner peace will follow.

Surrounding you with love. Ho'oponopono ~ I love you, I'm sorry, Please forgive me, Thank you.

A Prayer for Peace
When Tempted to Panic

Lysa Terkeurst

Father God, I know it is normal for us
sometimes to find ourselves in a pit of
fear and discouragement.
But we don't have to stay there.
Today, we're choosing to fix our eyes on You.
And we're remembering that each thing we verbalize
our thankfulness for is like
a stepping stone out of the pit we've been in.
Thank You for providing Your timeless truths
that prove to us over and over again
how powerfully capable You always are.
With You by our side, we have no need to fear.
In Jesus' Name,
Amen.

Be Still

AND KNOW THAT I AM GOD
— PSALM 46:10 —

An Everyday Path to Peace
by Cherie Flinn Clark

Every morning, before my feet touch the floor, I choose peace. Not because life is free of pain—it isn't. My body aches deeply, sometimes relentlessly. Yet I hold the promise close: by His stripes, I am healed.

Jesus didn't die only for salvation; He died for my healing, wholeness, and peace. That truth steadies me when chaos rises and suffering presses in. There is a peace not from this world but from the heart of God: "And the peace of God, which surpasses all understanding, will guard your hearts and minds in Christ Jesus" (Philippians 4:7).

It is not always easy, but I practice that peace daily. I begin with rest, letting my body recover. I wake slowly, offering gratitude before complaints. I meditate on His Word, letting it reframe pain with promise. I nourish my body as I'm able, and I move, sometimes gently, with great effort but always with love.

I sit in silence to hear the still, small voice that calms my soul. I avoid what drains my spirit and surround myself with love, laughter, and support. I serve when I can because love often flows strongest when it costs something. And I laugh, especially with my grandchildren, because joy is holy.

Some days are hard. Still, I focus on what I want: peace, healing, love, and not on what's missing. I remind myself, this too shall pass. I seek beauty, breathe gratitude, and hold fast to truth. The greatest of these is love—loving God, others, myself, and the life I've been given. Pain may visit, but peace lives here. That peace holds, heals, and carries me forward with hope. Peace isn't a destination; it's a daily choice.

Make every effort to live in peace with everyone.

Hebrews 12:14

Finding Peace in Surrender

April Mastey

Sometimes, God guides us through the deepest valleys, knowing we will either seek Him in ways we never have or find ourselves lost on paths we were never meant to walk. Our youngest son, Kane, now 8, was born with Mosaic Trisomy 18, or Edwards Syndrome. His journey has been one of relentless hardship, yet it has also led us to a peace we never thought possible.

Kane's first 227 days were spent in hospitals, where every breath he took felt like a fragile gift. Each time he battled a crisis, we prayed desperately, pleading for his survival. And still, we give thanks daily—for the life we've been given, no matter how difficult.

The next few years brought countless hospital stays, surgeries, and doctors' appointments, leaving us yearning for normalcy. Our family was divided. I stayed at a Ronald McDonald house an hour away, managing Kane's care and my business, while my husband, Patrick, balanced his work and cared for our two young sons.

Through these trials, we learned that true peace is not found in the absence of suffering, but in surrendering control. It was in the darkest moments—when our son fought for his life—that we found peace that surpassed all understanding. We witnessed miracles that only God could orchestrate.

True peace, we've discovered, is a gift from God, born not from an easy life, but from trusting that He is in control. This peace calls us to seek more, to trust more, and to love more deeply—even through the hardest of days.

Peace Through Pain Brings Joy

Catherine Laakso

The vision, so clear in my mind, of Jesus' arm reaching toward my Sissy Boo, is my peace. The moment I learned she had passed, Jesus blessed me with my vision—one of my most beautiful gifts from GOD. I am so grateful. Learning that my sister had gone home with Jesus was a shock. I immediately heard "Charlie Brown" voices of "wonk wonk wonk" with zero attention to any details.

Jesus knows. HE knew I'd be completely shattered and paralyzed with devastation. Jesus loves us all so much and is IN all the details. HIS arm had a white, billowy sleeve, and pure glowing light surrounded it, while HE was bringing her home. This vision is my peace.

Pure Love. Pure Joy. Pure Perfectness.

I saw her lifted, and peace came over me.

Jesus is Peace.

Days have passed, and earthly grief sets in. Sissy Boo deserves every tear. To love, and to be loved, this much is a privilege. Sisters are special and have unique bonds that glue us together. Yes, even the turbulent teenage years hold special bonds. They are still bonds.

Thank you, Jesus, for blessing me with my Sissy Boo for 63 years. Thank you, Jesus, for giving me the vision of you taking her home.

I saw her lifted, and peace came over me.

Jesus is Peace.

"Blessed are those who mourn,
for they will be comforted."

Matthew 5:4

Sanctuary

by KB

I stand alone, frozen in fear, trapped in a mall
Trapped in this sea of mingling souls
Their words are burning with gossip
My energy completely controlled; I could feel their tight grip on my
silver marionette strings.
Like the shops beckoning for consumption

The melodic cackles echo across the walls, piercing into my temples
Deafening to my covered ears
Every time I open my eyes, I can only see saturated blurs: orange,
neon green, electric purple.
My skin, my very nerves, buzzing like TV static

I want to scream, to cry, to break free, but the desperation gets caught
in my dry throat.
Nothing but turmoil, on the impasse between who I want to be
And how I am perceived in this world
I can only whimper

Before I shut down, I suddenly feel myself sprint away from the
food court,
A glimmer of hope propelling me forward

To my relief, the automatic gates open, and I fly up to my hilltop home
The soft verdant carpet welcoming against my legs; the misty gust
cool against my skin
I returned to my cocoon, the comforting darkness greets me
Soft stars aglow

For the first time in a long time, I feel a sense of peace in my heart

I'm greeting myself like I would a best friend after having a bad dream
In the care of someone who understands my very being

I look out my window and see the outside world
Realizing the struggles that others go through in their human experience
Their day-to-day lives
I understand now, details I never noticed before

And I began to wonder…When midnight arrives and the mall closes…
Does it get quiet, does the bustle fade?
Does it become a sanctuary, too?

Afterword

Gratitude Brings Peace
Through the Storms of Life

by John G. Falcon, MD

I magine you find yourself 100,000 miles away in the void of space. Out in the heavens, you gaze upon a magnificent orb we call home. You stand mesmerized by a vibrant cerulean sphere that is punctuated by streaks of ethereal pearl white clouds. The continents leap out defiantly from the sea. A brilliant halo of light encompasses the Earth like a diamond in the sky. What is even more breathtaking is the infinite expanse beyond the Earth. It is resplendent with scintillating stars whose numbers transcend comprehension. There is perfect order. Everything has a purpose. In that moment, you realize you are peering at the face of God.

Now imagine you are zooming into the Earth. You zoom past the haze of the clouds and cities, towns, villages, and countryside come into focus. Anonymous people are hustling Helter Skelter like ants on a mound; there is chaos everywhere. Eight billion people inhabit the Earth. Eight billion souls. It is easy to feel lost among eight billion people. It is even easier to feel insignificant. So many of us wander through life without purpose. In those rare moments of solitude, we wonder, "Why are we here?"

We live in a materialistic society, and we have been indoctrinated to believe that our purpose exists out there in the realm of things. We are seduced to externalize our dreams and believe that we must find the perfect life, the perfect partner, and the perfect job. The ads on television assure us that a luxury car, a big home, or a cruise to the Caribbean will set us free. Never mind if you cannot afford any of those things. It is all an illusion.

People tend to focus on what they do not have. Their sense of lack becomes the center of their being. Most fall into a profound depression if they perceive that they do not have enough money, love, hope, celebrity, purpose, or peace. As a result, far too many turn to pills for their salvation. The House of Medicine is guilty of peddling fool's gold. I have been practicing as an emergency physician for 35 years; nearly every day, I attend to patients who suffer the aftermath of that fallacy. Nonetheless, the solutions from most psychiatrists is to prescribe more medications.

I believe that staying in a state of gratitude is the essence of finding true peace. I have been blessed as an emergency physician. Daily, I encounter significant instances of chronic illness, tragedy, and hardship. I must stand by and witness the devastation suffered by families who have lost a loved one. There is never any consolation for them. When I am having a bad day, I look at my 24-year-old patient who is quadriplegic. I imagine what it would be like if I could not move my arms or legs or could not even use the bathroom on my own. I would feel like a prisoner in my own body. There are countless others, the 32-year-old man with the stroke who's left paralyzed and cannot speak, or the five-year-old child who was struck by a motor vehicle and left brain dead. Then there is the 65-year-old lady who is drowning in the fluids in her lungs due to congestive heart failure. I could go on ad nauseam, but you get the point. Amid that calamity, I stop to take a deep breath and recite a prayer of thanks. Instantly, I feel a sense of calm and am embraced by God's grace.

I will not lie to you and tell you that my life has been perfect. It has been anything but that. As a young man, I witnessed and dealt with the horrors of war. I also lived through a financially and emotionally devastating divorce; the scars and ramifications of which are still present today. When we had three daughters attending college at the same time, I was defrauded out of $250,000 by someone who I thought was a friend. I have been targeted by individuals and lost jobs because I will always stand up for the truth.

When Teresa Velardi asked me to write the afterword for *A Daily Gift of Peace* (something which I consider a great honor), I told her that I was struggling with the content because, currently, I am embroiled in a fight for medical freedom. I am living with considerable uncertainty on many fronts. Right now, I am walking through a dark tunnel and do not yet see the light on the other side.

It occurred to me that this is the perfect time to write about some of my life experiences. It is in our darkest moments that we need the greatest faith. I will tell you that without God and my faith, I would not have survived. I would not have been whole. God is ever present, and God watches over us. Whether we know it or not, the hand of God touches us.

During the Gulf War as a medical officer, I had an experience that changed my life. Soon after the ceasefire, I was given a critical mission. My orders were to inspect the medical readiness of the First Armored Division just after they arrived in Kuwait. My medic and I set off in a Humvee to cross twenty-five miles into the desert. The moment we left our unit, a vicious sandstorm bombarded us. We could not see three feet in front of us. It was as if we were driving through a Buffalo blizzard, except this time it was not a whiteout, it was a brownout. Due to the critical nature of the mission, I instructed my medic to continue driving blindly. Approximately 15 minutes into the trip, I heard a shrill voice in my right ear that screamed, "STOP!" I do not hear voices. I had never heard that voice before and have not heard it since. Instinctively, I yelled at my driver to stop the vehicle. When we came to a sudden halt, the wind died down and the sand settled. I could see for miles, and there was nothing but sand and the horizon.

My driver stared at me as if I were crazy for making him stop. Even so, I felt something was wrong. I instructed my driver not to move an inch as I stepped out of the vehicle. When I looked down, I saw an armed Rocket Propelled Grenade resting on the ground six inches away from our front right tire. If we had traveled six more inches, my driver and I would not be here today. Like a jolt from heaven, the hand of God saved us. I cannot say whose voice that was, whether it was my guardian Angel or a loving family member who had passed, but I can say that God did not intend for me to die that day.

Once you have been touched by the hand of God, it is impossible to look at life the same way. God watches over us always. We were granted the gift of free will, and as such, we are responsible for our choices. Our thoughts direct our choices, and they impact our reality. Most people do not understand the power of our thoughts, whether they are positive or negative. For some, it is easier to relinquish their power and live their life as if they were cascading down a raging river. That way, they do not have to take responsibility for life; they blame the river.

When people lose their way, they look at life through the lens of a microscope. The world becomes involuted, and they magnify negative emotions such as fear, hate, anger, bitterness, despair, or betrayal. Life, as they see it, becomes engulfed in endless darkness. No amount of money, drugs, or alcohol will deliver those souls from that abyss.

When we live in a state of gratitude, we experience God's unconditional love. Everything changes. Our hearts and minds become open to the abundance of the universe. God speaks to us in whispers. Through gratitude, those whispers become echoes from the mountain tops guiding us. Once we acknowledge that we are blessed with everything we need to survive and that we are abundant in spirit and love, the universe rewards us with abundance. Living with gratitude allows us to find joy in the simplest of things and in the quietest of moments. We understand that a small act of kindness can impact another soul for life. Those small acts that we believe go unnoticed ripple through the universe like a pebble tossed in a pond. Instead of looking at the world through a microscope, we look inward and travel 100,000 miles into space so we can once again marvel at the face of God. It is in that place where we find our purpose.

A Daily Gift of Peace is a collection of life experiences rendered by heroes. The authors courageously reveal how they took control of their lives. It reminds us that we as individuals do not live life in a vacuum. Our battles with adversity are not unique; we all come to learn universal truths. Our souls are interwoven in a magnificent tapestry that we call humanity. We share our stories so they may become a light for those of us in the abyss. May our stories fill those lost souls with hope and bring them home.

MATTHEW 5:14

I will both lay me down in peace, and sleep: for thou, LORD, makest me to dwell in safety.

Psalm 4:8

Resources for Peace
and Harmony

Books

- **The Power of Now** — Eckhart Tolle
  Mindfulness and presence to find peace in the present moment.

- **The Book of Joy** — Dalai Lama & Desmond Tutu
  Wisdom on happiness through compassion and resilience.

- **Sacred Rest** — Dr. Saundra Dalton-Smith
  Guidance on rest, renewal, and self-care.

- **Emotionally Healthy Spirituality** — Peter Scazzero
  Integrating faith and emotional well-being.

- **Wherever You Go, There You Are** — Jon Kabat-Zinn
  Practical mindfulness meditation for daily life.

Apps & Online Resources

- Insight Timer
- Free meditation app with guided sessions for all traditions.
- Calm
- Tools for meditation, sleep, and relaxation.
- YouVersion Bible App
- Scripture, devotionals, and daily encouragement.
- Headspace
- Mindfulness and stress-management techniques.
- DailyOM
- Inspirational courses on spirituality and wellness.

Organizations & Support

- Celebrate Recovery
- Christ-centered healing community for emotional and spiritual growth.
- National Alliance on Mental Illness (NAMI)
- Support and education for mental health.
- The Center for Action and Contemplation
- Teachings on contemplative spirituality and social justice.
- Mind & Life Institute
- Research on mindfulness and science for well-being.

Retreats & Spiritual Centers

- The Abbey of Gethsemani (Kentucky)
- Omega Institute (New York)
- The Billy Graham Training Center at The Cove (North Carolina)
- Spirit Rock Meditation Center (California)
- Mindfulness meditation and Buddhist teachings.

Daily Practices to Explore

- Meditation & Breathwork: Start with 5 minutes focused on breath or guided meditation.
- Prayer & Reflection: Use scripture, affirmations, or silent prayer to center yourself.
- Journaling: Write down daily gratitudes, emotions, or prayers.
- Nature Connection: Walk, garden, or simply be outdoors to refresh your mind.
- Acts of Kindness: Small intentional acts to foster harmony with others and yourself.

Front Cover
Contributing Authors

Alyssa Ruge is an award-winning attorney with over 20 years of public and private experience. She is admitted before the Supreme Court of the United States and the Florida Bar to practice law. Alyssa graduated from Stetson University College of Law in 2003 with her Juris Doctor, where she was a member of the Stetson Law Review. She is also a graduate of the University of South Florida, where she obtained her Bachelor of Arts degree in Political Science in 2001. She recently became a licensed foster parent in Florida and encourages others to become foster parents.

Amanda Beth Johnson is an intuitive healer, spiritual guide, and catalyst for transformation. Known for her ability to hold sacred space and channel profound inner clarity, she supports soul-led individuals in reconnecting to their power, purpose, and peace. Through her holistic approach, Amanda helps you align your energy, trust your inner wisdom, and rise into your next evolution with grace. If you're ready to return to your truth and live from a place of grounded magic, connect with Amanda and explore her offerings at: https://amandabethhealing.com/linktree amandabethhealing.com

Amy Olmedo is on a mission from God. Her first goal is to publish *White Heron: A Creation Story*, a blend of spirituality, mythology, and life lessons that inspire triumph over tragedy. Explore her journey by purchasing the book, visiting her website, and joining her community at www. whiteheron.us. Amy's second goal is to create a retreat where nature becomes a sanctuary for healing and self-discovery. Amidst mystical woodland trails and a honey bee farm, guests can rest, reconcile the past, and recreate their future, embracing the transformative power of nature and inner wisdom.

Dr. Anne Worth Anne Worth, MA, EdD, LPC, is a Christian author, counselor, and speaker. She has a mother's heart and has "adopted" children from all over the world, some are the four-legged kind. Her books include Call Me Worthy and a Christian children's book series entitled Tessie's Tears. Dr. Anne writes tracts and conducts workshops in schools, churches, and businesses, helping people write their personal mission statements. She volunteers at several organizations that give marginalized people a second chance. She shares God's love with whoever she can, as often as she can, and wherever she can! Learn more at http://www.dranneworth.com/

Denise C. Herndon Harvey is the published author of, "Growing up Sassafras -Where is my Daddy?" and "Emergence of Me - Discovering My Identity and Courage Within," She is also a contributing author of four other Amazon Bestselling books and has a new journal coming out soon called Emergence of Me – Discovering Your

Identity and Purpose Within. Denise is a graduate of Liberty University, holding an MA in Human Service Counseling – Family Advocacy and a BA in Psychology, with concentrations in Christian Counseling and Crisis Counseling. She and her husband have been married for over 41 years.

Donna Guary is a California children's author and Air Force veteran. Author of *"Broccoli! It's My Favorite Vegetable"* and *"Where in the World Does Broccoli Come From?"*, she weaves history into stories encouraging children to love vegetables. A contributor to the *"Daily Gift Book Series,"* she's pursuing her MA in Leadership.

Fran Asaro is a YouTube Mentor and Strategist. She is the Founder of the Senior Tuber Community where she helps mature people become well-versed YouTube Content creators as she walks them through the steps to leave their legacy, earn additional income, and share their gifts with the world. For more info visit: https://services.seniortuber.com/allservices or https://services.seniortuber.com/senior-tuber-circle

Gloria Sloan, founder and CEO of Personal Dynamics, Inc., has over four decades of experience in personal development, human resilience, and leadership service. Her expertise has empowered countless individuals to harness essential life skills for personal and professional growth. With a strong strategic business management and human resources background, Gloria delivers impactful international coaching and mentoring. As a dynamic speaker and facilitator, she inspires transformative self-discovery and growth by offering clear, practical approaches aligning core values with goals. An award-winning author, Gloria's *"Life Skills for the Journey"* is in its second edition. She hosts The Gloria Show podcast and contributes to Brainz Magazine and the *Daily Gift Book Series.*

Ilene Gottlieb,"The Heart Healer," is a Holistic Nurse, Spiritual Mentor, and Intuitive Guide with over 50 years of experience blending science and spirituality. She helps clients heal trauma, embrace self-love, and align with their soul's purpose through Vibrational Healing, Akashic Records Readings, and her signature Inner

Child Integration Process. Certified in Healing Touch, Medical Intuition, Quantum Healing, and Ho'oponopono, Ilene, a proud Trekkie, inspires others to "boldly go" where their soul calls. Founder of The Heart Healers Ho'oponopono Community, an International speaker, and bestselling contributing author, Ilene invites you to ask, "What is my most loving choice?" and follow that wisdom home to your heart.
https://linktr.ee/ilenegottlieb.thehearthealer

January Liddell a dedicated financial professional with over three years of experience, helps clients achieve tax-free gains and financial security through her ERFT method: "Eliminating Risk, Fees, and Taxes." Guided by Christian values, January protects her clients' hard-earned money from market volatility, ensuring peace of mind and long-term success. She is the author of *Alina, The Super Saver,* and co-host of the Sexy Freedom Media Podcast. Married to a retired veteran and mother of two, January enjoys boogie boarding, archery, and church. Her positive energy, financial expertise, and unwavering commitment make her a trusted ally in financial planning. Learn more at: www.januaryliddell.com.

Kathleen O'Keefe-Kanavos aka *Kat-The Queen of Dreams,* Host/Producer of Wicked Housewives On Cape Cod ™, *The Dreaming Healing* Video Podcast, guest on Dr. OZ, *BIZCATALYST360* "Living Your Dream," and *Desert Health* columnist, Dreamy Writers Conference Cruise facilitator, WEBE Books Editor, Author/Lecturer, Award winning, international bestseller, who promotes patient advocacy, and connecting with Inner-guidance through Dreams. www.KathleenOkeefeKanavos.com

Mark Heidt is an award-winning writer, director, producer of $30 Million in half-hour infomercials. He has a BS from Syracuse University and the State University of NY College of Environmental Science and Forestry. He has performed music at Carnegie Hall and fought forest fires in Idaho. Mark is the husband of Sandy, the father of  Ken and Ruth, and the grandfather of Graeme. He has a unique perspective on the influences that enlighten, empower, and motivate people to take effective action. His faith is above all.

Mariena Johnson is a 19-year-old law student at Cooley Law School expected to graduate in 2026. She received her Bachelor of Arts degree in Criminology from the University of South Florida in 2023 at the age of 17. She was a Team USA member for inline speedskating and attended the World Championships in Italy in 2023, where she skated the marathon race. She was a member of the Lumina Youth Choirs and performed at Carnegie Hall in New York City.

Mary Vovers Brown, founder of TriMedia3, helps small business owners reach their best customers. Her corporate background has honed her communication, strategic planning, problem-solving, and creativity skills. Originally from Australia, Mary has been fortunate to live  and work throughout the US. Her goal is to spread as much positivity into the world as possible. She is the proud single mother of two incredible souls. Reach her at: mary@trimedia3.com

Meredith Woolverton is a mother of four who transitioned from welfare to work. She holds a bachelor's in psychology and a master's in business. She is a published author in "Wake Up Women Be You Spread Your Wings and Fly" (Career and Finance) and is currently writing her full story expecting to publish it in the next year or so. mailto:mwoolverton@thejobsquad.com

Patricia Giankas walks in faith and grace, carrying a deep belief that every challenge holds the seed of transformation. With a heart rooted in compassion, she guides others to see possibility where there is pain, light where there is doubt, and hope where there is fear. Drawing on her wisdom and life experience, she inspires new beginnings, helping people trust the timing of their journey and embrace the  beauty within every season of life. Patricia reminds us that even in our most difficult moments, we carry the power to heal, grow, and create a life rich in peace, purpose, and abundance.

Peggy Willms is a certified trainer, sports performance nutritionist, health and wellness coach with over 35 years of experience spanning the medical, fitness, and corporate wellness industries. She is a radio show and wellness retreat host, and founder of All Things Wellness, LLC to include her trademarked All Things Wellness Wheel™ which exemplifies her holistic methodology, integrating nutrition, fitness, mindset, and behavioral change.http://www.allthingswellness.com/ mailto:peggy@allthingswellness.com

Rutez Mason, a native of New Orleans now resides in Keller, TX, walks boldly in her divine calling as Director of Health & Wellness, First Lady, mentor, and minister. She is the prophetic voice behind *I AM LOVED* and the forthcoming *The Player, The Preacher, & The Ponk...BUT GOD*, releasing September 1, 2025, on Amazon. Founder of  Jazzy Tazzy Kids, Rutez nurtures generations. Mother to Frederick, Destin, Elijah; bonus mom to Tywon; godmother to Joseph and Rodd; "grandtee" to Chris'Siana, Christopher, Christian, Case'Yiana; and grandmother to Markenzi. Alongside her husband, Pastor Bradford LeViege, she ministers healing, hope, and restoration.

Sally Mary de Leon is a U.S. Army Veteran, nurse, Mindvalley certified life coach, and advocate for resilience and peace. She has overcome poverty, domestic abuse, single parenthood, and loss, transforming each challenge into a stepping stone for growth. With an AAS degree in Paralegal Studies and VUCA certification, she blends practical tools with heartfelt inspiration. From serving her country to guiding others toward purpose, Sally Mary's mission is clear: to help people embrace stillness, live with intention, and choose peace daily. She believes peace is not found — it is created, one courageous choice at a time. Let's connect: www.sallymary.com

Rev. Maj. Sandra Kitt retired US Army Major, minister, author, coach, served during Desert Storm. In 2011, Neuroleptic Malignant Syndrome left her paralyzed. She now walks, talks, drives, swims, skis, is part of the First Unity Ministry team in St. Pete, Fl. and helps people thrive. Watch for Sandra's book **A Wink and A Prayer: A Veteran's Near Death Miracle** coming soon. http://www.RevMajSandraKitt.com

Sharlotte Brian is the author of *Prophetic Writings: Secrets from My Prayer Closet* and *Do You See What I See: True Stories of My Prophetic Visions*. Her books, available on Amazon, highlight her encounters with angels, OBEs (Out of Body Experiences), and prophetic visions, sprinkled with humor. For nearly 10 years, she has shared inspirational writings in her weekly column, 'Words from Above,' in the Pointe Coupee Banner Newspaper. Sharlotte's story appears in several books, and she participates in podcasts and book-signing events. Her upcoming book, *Hopelessly Devoted to You: A 365 Day Devotional to Jesus Christ*, is set to release in the fall of 2025.

Sherry Martin Peter spent her formative years as a missionary kid in Bolivia, where childhood meant riverbank adventures, learning Spanish, and hopping Cessna flights into the jungle. This unconventional upbringing sparked her passion for God, love of travel, and ability to find peace in life's storms—no matter how fierce.

 **Will Pollock** is a freelance multimedia journalist, researcher, and author in Atlanta. He's a contributor to TrumpFile.org and founder of CrankyYank.com, an online news magazine. A native of New York City, now domesticated in the South, Will is a proud dad to Cameron and Jackson, a Rat Terrier puppy. He's a lifelong tennis player and fan of The New York Yankees, despite the scourge of Alex Rodriguez. Will's fundraising effort, ARTvision Atlanta, and book Pizza for Good have raised over $100,000 for various charities.

"Peace is not something to wish for.
It is something you make,
something you are,
something you do and
something you give away."

Robert Fulghum

Contributing Authors

 **Alysia Lyons** is a Master Neuro-transformation Results Coach, Mom Support Coach, author and a Podcast host. As the proud mother of a son who has been her own course corrector, she now leads parents through long-lasting neurological shifts to help ease their guilt and increase their emotional peace to find their happy.

Born in the Bronx, NY, **Andrea Giammolvo** was the product of a musical family. She was raised on the hits of her first cousin Dion (Dion and the Belmonts), who visited often, sharing his love of the business - sparking Andrea to put her talents on the stage! She toured for 20 years, then created, wrote, and performed in her labor of love, *Sister Act Show- A*  *Historic Salute To The Divas,* which brought her to retirement! Andrea and her husband Andy have been extensively traveling, and enjoying their children and three beautiful grandchildren.

 **Angela Bertone**, with 30+ years of Bible study, has found the effect of unhealthy emotions on the body. Angela says, "God created the body perfectly for it is made in His image." She teaches that the body must tell the truth, including any lies that are held as truth. Many report signs, wonders, and miracles accompany her as she speaks the Word of God with divine power.

Angi Currier is a best-selling author and medical Patient Access Representative. She has three children (one passed from suicide) and two granddaughters. She hopes to inspire others with her triumph over addiction. Angi feels  like she has lived two lives. The first life involves physical and emotional struggles, and the second is living in gratitude, acceptance, and confidence. ajhinkle5@yahoo.com

In painting and a writing, we perceive our own reality, a glimpse of life's intangibility – the dark, the light, the movement, the continuance. From that perception, **Anne O'Brien** abstracts outcomes, without interference from the real, reflecting universality, individuality, emotion. That gives her work life and movement, evoking a world of one's own interpretation.

April Mastey is a devoted wife to Patrick, and mother of three boys, Noah (12), Cole (11), and Kane (8). Founder of Mastey Financial Group with 30 years in wealth management, she balances family, faith, and business while navigating her son Kane's medical journey. Rooted in Christ, April embraces gratitude, peace, and strength in every season of life.

Barbara Yager is a retired corporate attorney, an author, and an Akashic Record Coach. She specializes in getting her clients to leverage their Core Powers to gain greater happiness, success, and satisfaction in life. www.akashicalignments.com

Beth Johnston is the oldest daughter in a large family; Beth Johnston was born into management! Beth has spent her professional years reorganizing existing companies using her practical and logical perspectives to help companies achieve their highest profit years. She is known for her keen listening skills and inspiring interview techniques, now shared on B.E.P. TALKS. Beth can be reached at info@beptalks.com.

Candi Parker is an artistic entrepreneur whose personal mission is to use her gifts and talents to support others in realizing and expressing their own heart's desires. She is a best-selling author, book and cover designer, graphic artist, and publisher of the international *Positive Tribe Magazine*. www.positivetribe.com
mailto:candi@parkerhousebooks.com

Carla Lee Johnston was living the so-called American Dream when a radical transmission shattered every illusion of identity, she ever perceived mattered, revealing *The Truth of our Creation DNA*. She now honors her sacred stewardship as a messagebearer, wayshower, and mirror for humanity's awakening—*walking the path of remembrance* of our epic love story.

 **Carolyn Ballenger**, an ordained New Thought Minister, blends her lifelong love of rhyme with teachings on Oneness and Unity. Her upcoming chapbooks, Oneness and Somehow, share her spiritual journey and healing from emotional abuse. She lives in Ocala, Florida, enjoying life with her two beloved grandchildren.

Candy Radford has spent the last 5 years finding her peace while being a mom to 5 adult children and a middle school English teacher. Candy loves using her experiences to help others. She has always believed strongly that God has a plan for her life, even through the darkest times, and that He works all things together for good for those who love Him!

 **Cathering Laakso,** believes that a little bit of imagination can sprinkle joy everywhere. Living in Florida, she loves tending her plants, creating fun characters, encouraging stories, and spending time with her family and friends. Catherine's upcoming children's book, *The Sprinkle Spreader,* encourages children to spread kindness like sprinkles everywhere.

Cherie Flinn Clark, an ordained minister, creates heartfelt, love-filled wedding ceremonies. A former housing director for women in domestic violence shelters, she embodies empathy and trust. Now a licensed Medicare agent, she guides seniors with clarity and care. Cherie treasures family, especially her grandchildren, and uplifts others with unconditional love.

Debra Costanzo founded 3 in 1 Fitness by D. L. Costanzo, LLC in July 2008, earning her health coaching certification through the Institute of Integrative Nutrition. Debra helps women over forty to incorporate mindful lifestyle changes, supporting them to live healthy, energetic lives. Debra resides in Charlotte, NC. www.3in1fitness.com

Dorchelle Spence is an author, certified writing coach, and motivational speaker, covering self-advocacy and cancer survival to self-worth and the power of shoes. Her books include the novel, *No Less Worthy*, and *Into the Gathering Clouds*, a memoir of survival incorporating faith, friends, and finesse. To know more visit: www.DorchelleSpence.com

Eileen Bild is CEO of Ordinary to Extraordinary Life, Founder of the Core Thinking Blueprint Method, Breakthrough S.P.A.R.K. Coach, Mentor, Author, Keynote Speaker and Internationally Syndicated Columnist. She holds a Masters in Transpersonal Psychology and is host for OTEL Talk. She helps others live their best lives and become unstoppable!

With degrees in Nuclear Engineering, **Glenis McEwen Moss** blends science, coaching, and faith to help others thrive. A wellness coach before losing her husband in 2019, she added widows' and relationship coaching, guiding others toward health, hope, and extraordinary relationships while sharing God's peace and promises worldwide with her husband, Dr. Gary Moss.

Pastor Jack Rehill has been married to his wife Patricia for 53 years and is the father to four children and grandfather to three. Jack is the author of *The Advocate & The Adversary*, and the soon to be released book entitled *The Mediator* slated for publication in the winter of '25.

Jessie Tieva is CEO of "Born Abel," the foundation named for her son, Abel, who was born with Trisomy 18. Born Abel features children worldwide in colorful children's books, bringing awareness to their various complex medical conditions. In just two years old, Born Abel has reached all 50 states and 10 countries throughout the world. Learn more at https://bornabel.org/

 **Jo Ann Walczak's** career spans three decades as a high school teacher, an English teacher in China, a women's Bible study leader, and a freelance writer for various devotions. A mother and grandmother, she is the author of a new book, *The Walk on Layton: 52 Modern Parables for Your Journey.*

Jen Reed's wish is that everyone gets to connect with this kind of person. To feel the way I have been lucky enough to feel, and to have been lifted out of the darkness. Someday I pray that he will really understand what a light in this world he really is.

 **Joannie Strickler** is a 43-year-old mother of three living her best life in Florida with her youngest son and rescue dogs. She loves and is regularly active in her church. Completely obsessed with coffee, highland cows and dolphins. She began writing after a many years' gap to fill her days since God forcefully retired her in 2012 with a massive stroke. Her philosophy "there are two ways to live your life: 1) as if there are no miracles, or 2) that everything is in fact a miracle." She prefers the latter of the two.

Johnny Tan is an Experiential Keynote Speaker, Executive Career & Life Coach, Mentor, Multi-Award-Winning and Bestselling Author, Talk Show Host, Social Entrepreneur, Founder & CEO of From My Mama's Kitchen® Organization and Words Have Power store, Publisher of "Inspirations for Better Living" digital magazine, and a REIKI Master Teacher & Healer.

Joyce Waring is a retired LPN and Special Needs Para-educator. She enjoys writing, reading, gardening, walking her Labrador, and spending time with her husband, children and grandchildren in Central Oregon's high desert. She is Chaplain for COFRW and an active member of Trinity Lutheran in Bend, OR.

Karen Mayfield is a bestselling author, speaker, metaphysical minister, Spiritual Life Coach, and founder of Wake up Women. Karen takes you into the world and brand of Wake up Women while guiding you through your process of waking up to your life of happiness, health & wealth, with Peace of mind to live the life you love.

Kate Rohauer lives in Sisters, Oregon. She has a master's in Christian counseling. She's the Founder of Royal Touch Grief Outreach, and a contact person for Parents of Murdered Children. A great-grandmother who loves family, friends, and her husband of 40 years. Enjoys photography, crafts and gardening.

Katerina Pappas (LadyMoon) was born in Philadelphia and raised in Greece. Her journey started at the David. A. Clarke School of Law followed by the Institute for Integrative Nutrition, and finally, receiving her teaching certificate in Kundalini yoga, from Yoga Farm Ithaca. After many years of collecting life experiences,  she is infusing all her lessons into her first true loves; creative writing and singing. You can find her children's books and original songs at: ladymoonsongbooks.com

Katharine Banman's determined purpose is to know TheLORD and be known by Him. In His love, let Him draw others to live in positioned peace, purposed with Him; the 'Zealous Zion Zeal' of Father God!

Kevin Stark is the founder of The AretePath — a leadership path for leaders, warriors, and everyday people to rise above mediocrity. Kevin spent more than 25 years coaching and guiding Navy SEALs and nonmilitary teams, coaching through intense environments and real-world challenges. He helps people discover virtue, purpose, and the "quiet strength" of living with integrity. www.aretepath.com

Kimberly Eddy is a web designer, author, and coffee aficionado helping women bring their calling to life online through practical beauty and authentic connection. She believes well-designed websites can change the world by amplifying messages that matter. A recovering productivity junkie, she embraces liturgical rhythms over hustle culture.

Laurie Rowland is a published author, poet, writer and lyricist. Coming soon is her first Children's book, *Wink, The Super Fast Fly*. Her love of nature, travel, community and music inspire her writing. Her self-deprecating humor makes her approachable, drawing the reader in.

Lindi Martin is a wife and mother to three. Their youngest being medically complex. She's been married to her husband, Shane, for over nine years. Their son, Major, would be turning nine this year, but they lost him in utero at 20 weeks of gestation. Their daughter, Gray, is seven and a half years old and youngest, Hutt, is three.

Linette Rainville is a passionate speaker, author, mentor, and movement leader. As the founder of Daughters United, a global mentoring and equipping ministry, she emboldens women to *Start Little and Dream BIG*—growing ministries, missions, and movements from the ground up. With a heart full of stories and sleeves rolled up from years of  hands-on outreach, Linette brings encouragement, wisdom, and real-life tools to women who are ready to step into their God-given callings. Whether online or in person, she creates spaces where women can gather, grow, and go change the world—for such a time as this.

Lucia Murphy is a dynamic creator and entrepreneur, passionate about travel, food, and adventure. As co-host of "Life with Lucia & Glynn," she shares exciting journeys with her audience. With a zest for life and a heart for new experiences, Lucia inspires others to embrace exploration and joy.

Maria Crane is an award winning Speaker, Author and Artist who helps transform hearts and lives through the power of God's love. She loves mining out the treasure in people and helping them to identifying limiting beliefs so they can renew their minds and live out their true identity in freedom and joy.

Mark Nelson O'Brien is the principal of O'Brien Communications Group https://obriencg.com/ a B2B brand-management and marketing firm he founded in 2004. He's also the co-founder and President of EinSource. And he's a lifelong writer. You can see all of his published work on Amazon.

Marla Hamann is Mom to two handsome young men, Emma Layne and RD (Roy Dell IV), and Grandma to Milly. Marla and Emma are the Authors of *Emma's Adventures* Children's Book Series, encouraging others with TARS to live their best lives. Proceeds benefit www. tarsawarenesstexas.org/

Martariesa Logue is a published author in A Daily Gift of Hope, A Daily Gift of Kindness, and Wellness G.P.S. She inspires others through faith-centered reflections and storytelling, sharing lessons in real life and discussing her journey as a rare disease warrior. She enjoys adventures with her daughter, beagle, and hedgehog, hiking to waterfalls, and more recently attending Saturday night worship at Mount Tabor House Group.

Dr. Mary Sanford has been writing since the second grade. She has a passion for Christ Jesus, speedy pens, and is perhaps the fastest two-fingered typist in Seattle. When she's not writing, she loves coaching her ADHD clients, baking, dancing, raising Golden Doodle puppies, traveling, and volunteering as Head Elf Mary with the Forgotten Children's Fund.

How do you describe a woman who understands the rigors of life more than most? **Michelle Harwood-Lange's** experience stretches the gamut of exquisite joy to some serious life lessons none of us will see, even over a lifetime. She has learned to pivot those negatives into positive strengths. As an author, artist, and inspiring thought  leader, her mission is to share her life through the power of the written word and visual art to enlighten minds and awaken souls.

 **Michelle Rene' Hammer,** MS, LCPC, a Certified Pastoral Counselor, BREAKTHROUGH Coach, motivational speaker, and bestselling author, helps women leaders navigate life's challenges in clinical and biblical ways. Her mission is to empower successful yet overextended Christian women to break through barriers to satisfying relationships and abundant joy-filled lives.

Michael Starr, executive coach and Navy veteran, built businesses and guided hundreds toward growth. His adventures—from canoeing 54 days to summiting Kilimanjaro at sixty-nine—shaped his philosophy of Betterism. His book, *Journey Into Peace*, teaches blending resilience, empathy, and exploration, inspiring others to seek more good and win-win outcomes. www.executivecoachingservices.net

 **Monica Talbot-Kerkes** is making her dreams of writing adventurous and educational children's books come true. Her vision is to inspire, teach, and positively impact children while bringing awareness to world crises and the amazing animals and places on our beautiful planet and the Solar System. Learn more at www.LloveLlama.com

Morgan Danielle is a love and relationship coach who helps ambitious women break toxic relationship cycles, heal their attachment wounds, and attract emotionally available, secure, partners. Her work empowers women to rebuild self-trust, embody their worth, and create the most epic, soul aligned love story of their lives from the inside out.

Dr. Rachelle Simpson Sweet is a certified epigenetic coach with a background in neuropsychology, specializing in personalized wellness through genetics. As an author and contributor to four books, she integrates mental, physical, and emotional health. Passionate about helping others thrive, she inspires them to embrace customized health solutions for optimal well-being. www.drrachellesweet.com

Rebecca Laird is a Creator and Connector, who, alongside her pastor husband, and three grown sons, is the founder of Grace Worship Arts in Arcade, NY. Born in Ontario, Canada, she has served the Lord in the United States since studying Ministry & Music at Elim Bible College, Lima, NY in 1994.

Renea Attaway is a Bible Teacher, Speaker, and Author with a background in healthcare and culinary arts. She is the CEO of Destiny by Grace Inc., a ministry dedicated to empowering individuals. With 35 years in ministry and 24 in business leadership, she helps others overcome challenges through faith and practical skills.

Ruth Holly Currey is the daughter of Mark and Sandy Heidt and the sister of Kenny Heidt. She lives in Orlando, Florida, with her 13-year-old son, Graeme. Valedictorian of her class at St. Petersburg HS, Ruth went on to receive her BA in Animation and MS in Education from UCF. She taught art in Orange County for 11 years and is now an Artist and Digital Planner. Ruth enjoys running and loves Disney.

Tammy Hader authored *Walking Old Roads: A Memoir of Kindness Rediscovered*. She is a regular contributing author in the Daily Gift Book Series and an essay writer at BizCatalyst360, Medium, and WebMD. You can find details about her published works at tammyhader.com.

Ted Jordan started his career in the entertainment industry in 1983 and has amassed an impressive resume. His work encompasses a diverse range of roles, including on-air radio DJ, model, on-camera TV commercials, voice-overs, acting coach, stage work, indie films, feature film work, writer, director, producer, and author.

Dr. Teresa Lynch, DPT, is a health coach and physical therapist dedicated to integrative healing. She blends functional nutrition, energy psychology, movement, and faith-based guidance to help women over 60 thrive. With compassion and expertise, Teresa empowers others to restore balance, cultivate resilience, and embrace vibrant, whole-person wellness.

Tyra Glaze is a proud mother to Tae & Que, a Breast Cancer Warrior, Educator, Author ("My Mom Is My Hero") & Founder of FIERCE Emporium, a faith-driven brand empowering women to live boldly. She has been featured on platforms such as Susan G. Komen and TORRID, inspiring others to fight with faith, embrace resilience, and stand in their power.

Meet the Author
Teresa Velardi

Teresa is a bestselling author, publisher, host of the *Conversations That Make a Difference* podcast, coach, and potter.

Michaelangelo, the famous 15th-century artist and sculptor said, *Every block of stone has a statue inside it, and it is the sculptor's task to discover it.* His job was to remove the excess stone to reveal the beauty within.

Similarly, Teresa uses the art of pottery to illustrate that each ball of clay can and will be transformed into a beautiful work of art with the touch of the potter's hand. Teresa guides her clients through the process of centering, molding, shaping, and walking through the fire of challenges to effect positive life change as they gracefully and powerfully embrace the work of art they already are.

Teresa found her passion and purpose through life's challenges while trusting God's plan. Faith in God, gratitude, and giving are her heart. Her abilities as a writer, editor, and publisher are vital ingredients she brings to those who share their message with the world on her podcast or through her publishing platform.

Her daily quiet time, writing, and gratitude practice keep Teresa focused on her God-given purpose as life unfolds in this ever-changing world. We all have a story to tell and a heartfelt message to share. What's your message?
https://linktr.ee/teresavelardi.

Meet the Foreword
Andi Buerger, JD

Andi is the Founder and Chair of Voices Against Trafficking™, an international nonprofit organization dedicated to ending human trafficking in the U.S. and abroad. She also co-founded Beulah's Place, another nonprofit which served at-risk homeless teens in danger of abuse, trafficking or other criminally predatory activities. Andi, herself a victim of unspeakable abuse, is a highly sought-after international speaker and advocate for those who cannot speak for themselves. Andi's books are available online at Amazon.com including her newest release, *Voices Against Trafficking - Courage Is Contagious.* Her magazine, *Voices Of Courage®* is available on VoicesOfCourage.media.

Andi is regularly heard across the airwaves and on television podcasts, speaking on Capitol Hill and for government agencies, universities, churches, businesses, and more in the U.S. and abroad. By sharing her personal story, Andi is creating greater awareness of human trafficking, child exploitation, and the devastating cost to America's future.

Meet the Afterword
John G. Falcon, MD

John was born in Cuba and immigrated to the United States with his family at the age of five years old. His family overcame atrocities that were committed by Fidel Castro's communist regime. Growing up, he learned from his parents to stand up for liberty and the truth. He graduated from Lemoyne College in Syracuse, NY, and attended Georgetown University medical school. He completed his residency in emergency medicine at the University of Southern California - Los Angeles County Medical Center.

Dr. Falcon was a medical officer with the Second Armored Cavalry Regiment during the Gulf War. He served three years of active duty and three years of reserve. He is a recipient of two Bronze Stars, one for valor, among other awards for his service during the Gulf War. For 35 years, Dr. Falcon has worked as an emergency physician in trauma centers and has educated countless medical students and residents in Charleston, South Carolina Scranton, Pennsylvania, and Spartanburg, South Carolina.

He is the author of an upcoming memoir about his experience in the Gulf War, *Shelter from The Storm.* He has been married to his wife, Deborah Lynn, for 30 years and has helped raise three beautiful daughters, Brittany, Danielle, and Sonja. Dr. Falcon is active in his community on many fronts and still fights for truth and justice.

Peace Story Take-Aways

Name of Story:

Author:

How I connected to the Story:

Peace Story Take-Aways

Name of Story:

Author:

How I connected to the Story:

Peace Story Take-Aways

Name of Story:

Author:

How I connected to the Story:

Peace Story Take-Aways

Name of Story:

Author:

How I connected to the Story:

Peace Story Take-Aways

Name of Story:

Author:

How I connected to the Story:

Peace Story Take-Aways

Name of Story:

Author:

How I connected to the Story:

Peace Story Take-Aways

Name of Story:

Author:

How I connected to the Story:

Next up in the Daily Gift Book Series

A Daily Gift of Friendship

Our friends are SO very Important in this journey we call "life."

Share a heartwarming story about a friend who has made a difference in yours.

Just in time for the Holidays 2025!

Have you, a friend or family member experienced cancer?

Whether you are/were the patient, caregiver, friend or relative, your story matters. Hope comes with experience.

Available on 2/4/26
World Cancer Day

A Daily Gift for a Peaceful Journey Through Cancer

Learn how you can be part of this life-changing series at
www.dailygiftbookseries.com

www.ingramcontent.com/pod-product-compliance
Lightning Source LLC
Chambersburg PA
CBHW051137120626
46547CB00012B/845